TRACe

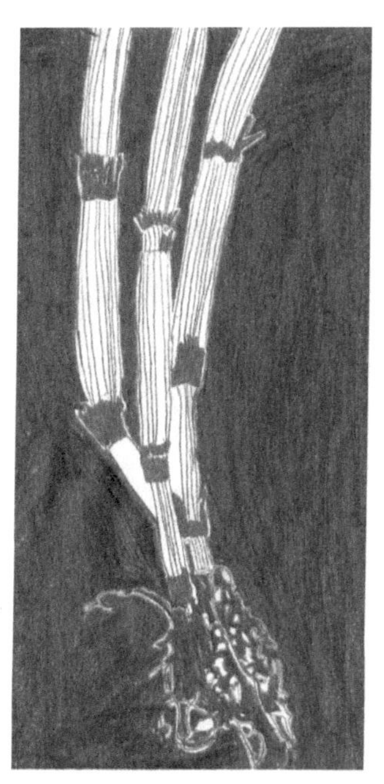

TRACe

by
ROMA TEARNE

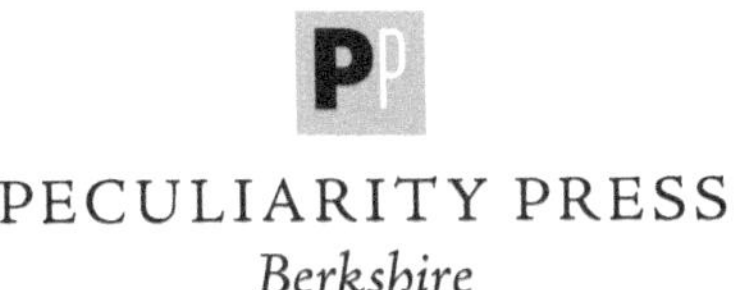

PECULIARITY PRESS
Berkshire

First published in 2023.

2nd edition.

ISBN 978-1-912384-18-1

PRINTED IN GREAT BRITAIN

For
Sue Parker
&
Lloyd Spencer

'… *when we die, what we lose is not the future*
but the past.'
Carlos Fuentes

PREFACE

TRACE IS relatively new on the museum scene. Privately funded, the concept of forming an institution of historical tracings has long been overdue. The idea originated some years ago when I, Emile Charpentier, was still the director of a much older, more traditional museum in the provinces.

◆

I received a trunk.

It came from an unknown donor. It was addressed to me personally and consisted of a collection of archival material. This included a bundle of letters, some objects and photographs. Almost all of it was in poor condition, water-damaged and undated. Amongst the objects and papers were also a few fragments of text from a book called *BEAUTÉS de l'histoire de France*. The book was one with which I was familiar, but currently no longer in print. Published in 1827, these discoloured pages sent to me were unfortunately of no value to any antiquarian bookseller or traditional museum in their current state. But I could not bear to throw them away and so I stored the entire trunk in the basement stack of the museum where I was working, until such time as I retired when I would be able to take a closer look at its contents.

These items now form the main body of what is now the TRACe Museum.

Other material has been sent to me since from the original donor's relatives, all of them relating in some way to the material in the original trunk. At this point, due to the growing number of items and because space had become an issue, I was forced to look for a suitable venue in which to house the collection. It had occurred to me that these items would form a most interesting museum and so I decided to look for a building. I spent a year looking for such a place but found nothing until a chance letter amongst some papers gave me this address. The house was for sale and the asking price reasonable on account of its run-down appearance. Within moments of walking in I knew it was exactly what I wanted. I put in an offer and it was accepted. In that moment, the TRACe Museum was born.

．

It took another year before I was ready to open the doors to the public but when I did the response was gratifying. Inevitably there was a vast outpouring of donations, of objects, letters and manuscripts offered to me by total strangers. Hundreds of photograph albums came my way too. Most were politely declined. I had, you see, a particular vision from which I would not budge.

It is therefore with great pleasure that I now welcome you, the visitor, to this vision.

◆

On entering you will be forgiven for thinking the items within these rooms appear to belong to one person alone. You will be mistaken in this, and on closer inspection it will become clear that the exhibits belong to everyone who has ever lived. It is my hope that what is on display is not dissimilar to those objects, photographs, the diary entries and notes-to-self, that are familiar to you.

Presenting them in a coherent and logical fashion within the confines of nine small rooms has been a considerable challenge. As custodian of the collection, it has been my aim to cross cultures and time simultaneously; to illuminate the connections that exist between the objects and the people who once owned them. To illustrate how both touch and thought never really disappear, showing how connections from a vanished past still matter to all of us today. The painstaking task of organising the material has been both rewarding and time-consuming.

Some exhibits may currently be absent, on loan to similar venues springing up in other places around the world. I have been careful to ensure that no more than three items are loaned out in this way at any given time as the chronological order of the story presented here should not be totally disturbed. It is of importance to me too that other similar museums in other countries should feel able to display their own collections in whatever way they wish, according to national bias or tradition. For in the end these human stories remain universally the same. One that is familiar to all.

Each room in the TRACe Museum has been ordered chronologically. It is useful, though not necessary, to begin your visit at the Entrance [clearly marked on the map.]

The rooms are as follows:
    Entrance
    Hallway
    Sitting Room
    Master Bedroom
    Child's Bedroom
    Bathroom
    Dining Room
    Kitchen Garden.

The objects present in these rooms have been chosen for several reasons, not all of them the same. Some are present because they were in the original trunk and are of sentimental value, some were donated by the trustees, others by migrants passing through to other worlds. Included are examples of objects created with extraordinary artistic skill

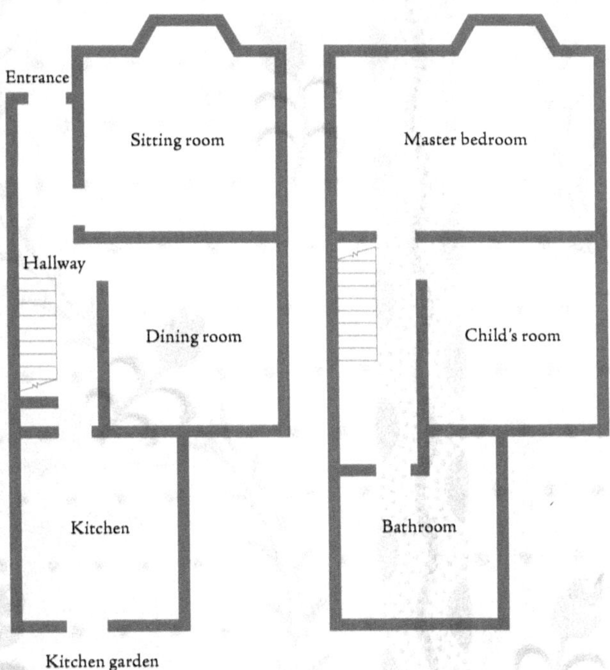

Entrance
Sitting room
Master bedroom
Hallway
Dining room
Child's room
Kitchen
Bathroom
Kitchen garden

or craftsmanship. Some found and partially destroyed objects are also represented. These unique fragile items, broken and badly mended, are rare historical survivors of a bygone era. Each might have a substantial provenance. Many bear witness to a significant historical moment, or document a series of events. All of them, without exception, tell fascinating stories about the cultures that produced them and the people who owned them. Often, they demonstrate the powerful external events that changed the ways in which individuals connected with each other and the surprising irrelevance of both time and place in the emotions of human experience. Experience that remains fundamentally unchanged.

•

This museum, the objects and the ideas within its walls have not, until now, received sufficient attention. But the past cannot be erased. The past is a text that, even if suppressed, will return to shape the lives of those left behind. In this struggle between remembering and forgetting there is always a constant danger of the latter disappearing completely. Thus, to save the forgotten is the aim of TRACe. The fragmentary and transient memories of inherited pasts can now gather together here, peacefully and finally, and exist beside the bustle and noise of current lives. What might be forgotten, or considered no longer relevant, can be seen together for the first time in its entirety.

I hope the visitor will delight in observing these connections. There are, of course, many other examples of lives and events that go back to earlier periods situated in this space, but it is currently not possible to show them all.

Please note:

Although no attendants or guides are present, CCTV cameras operate throughout the building at all times.

There are several explanatory leaflets at the entrance to each room. These are free. The audio recordings can be purchased in advance of your visit [see website below] and will, I hope, enhance the experience of the visit. There is no entrance fee although donations can be left in the box provided at the front door. All proceeds from the sales of the recordings will go towards the upkeep of the museum.

If this is your first visit, I hope you will be inspired to return to spend some time in meditation within these rooms. I would like to think of this place as an eternal space, a place where time itself disappears, and the past and those who peopled it live on in the visitor's imagination. What more can a museum hope to achieve, than this?

One final note. There is no tearoom at TRACe. To save any disappointment it is also necessary to state that there is no shop either. There are no tote bags for sale, no pencils, ceramic mugs, tea towels or trinkets of any kind. On leaving, the visitor can be certain only of one thing: that which can be carried in the imagination is all that matters, as only this is forever transportable into other lives. If this should disappoint, might I politely suggest that this is not the museum for you?
Yet.

Professor Emile Charpentier.
Director, TRACe, 2022.

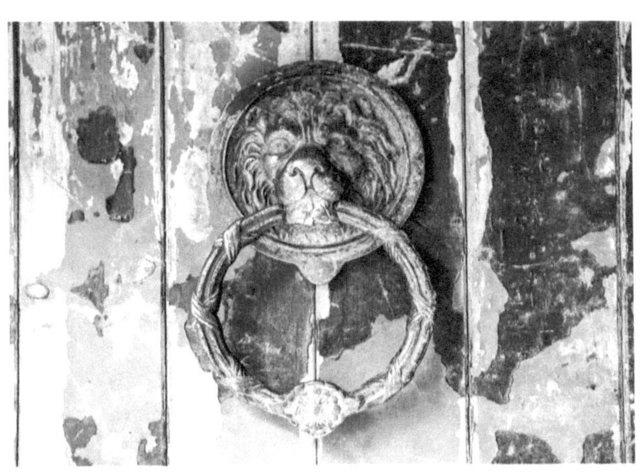

CONTENTS

Frontispiece

Root

I

THE ENTRANCE

THE DOOR is black. In order to see it clearly the visitor will need to begin engaging with their imagination. Some things remain hidden in plain sight. The front garden is not neglected; appearances are nearly always deceptive. If you are visiting in winter rest assured that there will be bluebells pushing their way up when spring returns. Also, in spring there will be clouds of cherry blossoms in the adjacent streets giving the whole area a Japanese feel. At that brief time the ground will be carpeted in blossom which the rain will soon wash away. In spring too, the huge old plane trees will be silent. They have been here for more than a hundred years and have grown to enormous heights. In summer they will shade the street and the sounds of birds will drift down from the branches. And if your visit is in the autumn the ground will be carpeted with their leaves, dying as the temperature drops.

For this museum and its environment are cyclic.

So now to the entrance.

Ring the bell and a buzzer will sound. When you walk into the vestibule with its black and white chequered tiles, you will see two bicycles. These belong to the people who no longer live here. What little light there is comes down from a window on the first floor. No one lives there either anymore, although it has to be said, occasionally footsteps can be heard moving restlessly around. There are three ghosts in the building. Two very old who, rumour has it, died a violent death, and one more recent. The old ghosts, one older than the other, live upstairs, each in their own self-contained apartment. Sometimes, they bang on the wall but never at the same time. The sound of each knocking is distinctly different.

◆

According to historical accounts, the first of the ghosts was that of a man born in 1885. This man, Walter Chrysostom, lived in the house until the age of 19. Then, having accepted the King's shilling, he went to war. He was reported missing in action. His mother, who lived in the house at the time, never got over his loss. She kept a photograph of him on her mantelpiece and would place fresh flowers beside it. As time passed, she developed a blood clot in one eye and began to go blind. The photograph of her boy hung over the mantelpiece and grew blurred with time. It was at this point her

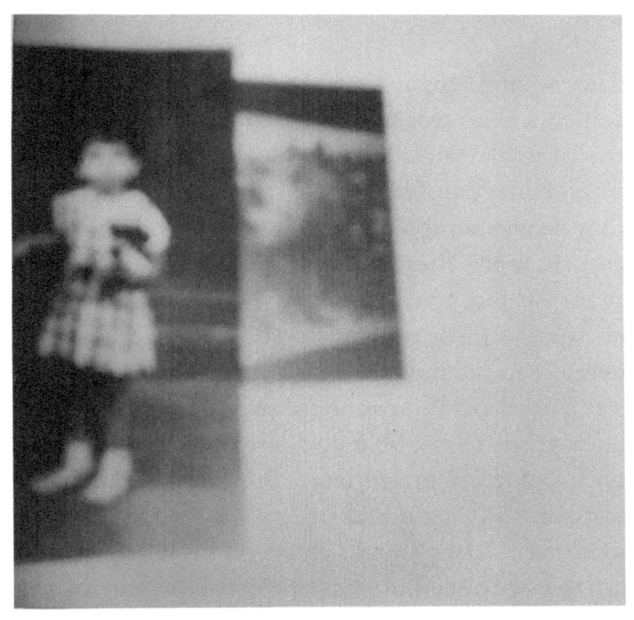

son began to tap on the wall. She believed it was to reassure her of his continued presence in her life. At her death the photograph was lost. We, at the museum, have replaced it with another. A stand-in, or understudy of the past.

+

The second apparition, so the story goes, was someone who worked in a property nearby during the Blitz of World War Two. The man's name was Theo [surname unknown]. It has been rumoured that he was some sort of undercover worker for the government. There is no other information other than the fact that Theo had tried to take shelter in the building during a sudden air raid. He never made it and was killed just on the corner of Southey Road. Someone subsequently dragged his body from the rubble and left it at the entrance of TRACe for burial later. But the air raid siren had sounded again and the passer-by had scurried to shelter. After the all clear the body had disappeared, with a single handprint appearing on the upstairs window. Every year, on September 18th, a faint handprint can be traced once again on the upstairs window. It is always the same print of a left hand.

+

The stairs leading to the upper floors are uncarpeted. The current occupants, out during the day, only contacted the staff at TRACe on one occasion. It was when I myself pasted a notice on the vestibule wall, beside the bicycles, declaring my intention of turning the property into a museum. This was a requirement of Lambeth Borough council for legal purposes, obviously. I was also advised to inform the occupants on the upper floor that there would be a number of visitors arriving regularly and therefore personal belongings left in this vestibule are done so at the owner's own risk. As soon as the woman in the first-floor apartment read the notice, she offered some material: photographs, letters, furniture, etcetera, to add to the existing archival material. On being told this was not what the museum was about and that it was an archive of invisible imprints, she demanded to know what kind of archive was that?

'It is an archive of what was lost,' I told her courteously. 'A collection of things that have been destroyed or misplaced for various reasons and have, with patience, been re-formed. Re-formed in ways that are not necessarily a recreation of the original but more the essence of past times.'

The woman was puzzled.

'How on earth is it possible,' she demanded, 'to represent what has been lost?'

'Ah!' I said, smiling, 'you should come and see for yourself. This museum is unique. The objects mostly belong physically to one migrant who

carried them across oceans. But over time every-thing was lost. Until it was re-found by sheer will-power by the generation that followed. It is the old story of those who have travelled restlessly around the world. It represents those precious things that the refugee frequently misplaces. One moment these objects, too precious to leave behind, were tied up in bundles, tucked into suitcases, folded carefully between the pages of books, and the next moment they had vanished. No amount of frantic searching, no amount of weeping, would bring them back. And the eternal question remained: how had they been lost?'

There are countless stories of refugee-loss and nearly always this loss is accompanied by a feeling of complete bewilderment.

•

Most museums resign themselves to becoming period pieces, putting much of their collections out on display. Others turn themselves into high-tech interactive theme parks and simply put most of their collections into storage. Archives are usually stored away in boxes, not set out as objects as you will find here.

For this reason our museum is unique.

II

THE HALLWAY

THE TASK of forming a new museum is an ambitious one. The visitor's experience needs to be an interesting one. Most national museums, by occupying magnificent buildings in enviable locations with untold riches on display, are perfectly capable of maintaining that interest. These museums enjoy great public support [no politician would dare to eradicate them, even in times of great hardship] and so the visitors keep coming. In this way all those impressive national archives, those keepers of the past, continue to flourish.

But such museums are also 'like trees in winter: their collections, like closed buds holding tight to their secrets… need to become more like trees in summer, with collections flowering in the minds of each visitor.' To be a repository for past thoughts and fading memories, not a few carefully selected comments that masquerade as facts on a label, are what is needed. And it is this gap in our museum market that we at TRACe wish to close. Do not be deceived by what you first see as you enter our hallway. For the Memory within these spaces is not always touchable.

Ursula's mother left her shoes in the hallway before turning left into her bedroom. She was tired, ready for sleep. How was she to know that it would be the long and final sleep that ended life? So it was, on that last evening, she left her small orange court shoes outside her bedroom door, right there in the hall. She would not be needing them again, not in this life at least. They stayed in the hallway until someone unknown to Ursula threw them away. But Ursula would carry a trace of those shoes around with her for the rest of her own life, carrying them year after year, making her heart heavy and her arms weary of the burden. Today they live on in our archive, a simple trace of a pair of shoes, living again as surely as the vaporised figure of the man sitting on the steps of the Sumitomo Bank in Hiroshima lives in the Peace Museum.

The shadow of those shoes, one turned inwards towards the other, indicated the manner in which Ursula's mother had stepped out of her life. The energy involved in pushing out the heel of her right foot had been the reason the left shoe was turned on its side. It had been part of a bedtime ritual, preparing for the night. She was, of course, unaware that this night would be her longest and the lack of foresight added to the poignancy of the gesture. Today there is a shadow etched along the skirting board against which the shoe rested. Look carefully, for although the hallway has been redecorated, cleaned up, carefully reconstructed, floorboard by floorboard, this reconstruction does not tell the full story. In fact, it might be argued that such renovation, however sensitively done, does not tell any story at all. What lies beneath the clean lines of heritage colours, one might ask? To which the answer can only be: the life of a migrant woman whose shoes tell something of the long journey she had undertaken across time.

A journey that ends as all journeys end.

◆

Why display a pair of vaporised shoes as the very first exhibit the visitor encounters on entering our museum?

Those shoes, depicting the exact moment time stopped and energy and motion froze for one individual. There is the single shoe turned towards the other, one foot leaving its life moments before the other. No other exhibit shows this more clearly. The shoes were both the first and last item Ursula's mother was to shed before leaving this world. The absence of a foot, rather like the empty chair drawn by a once unknown painter, signifies loss.

Another good reason for putting this object on show in its fragmented form is to enable more people to have the chance to understand, from the inside out, the story of this archive. Loss is all around TRACe. It begins in the blank wall that meets the visitor on entering, in the shoes that will never be worn again, the shoes that only exist as a trace.

The narrowness of the hall adds to this sense of

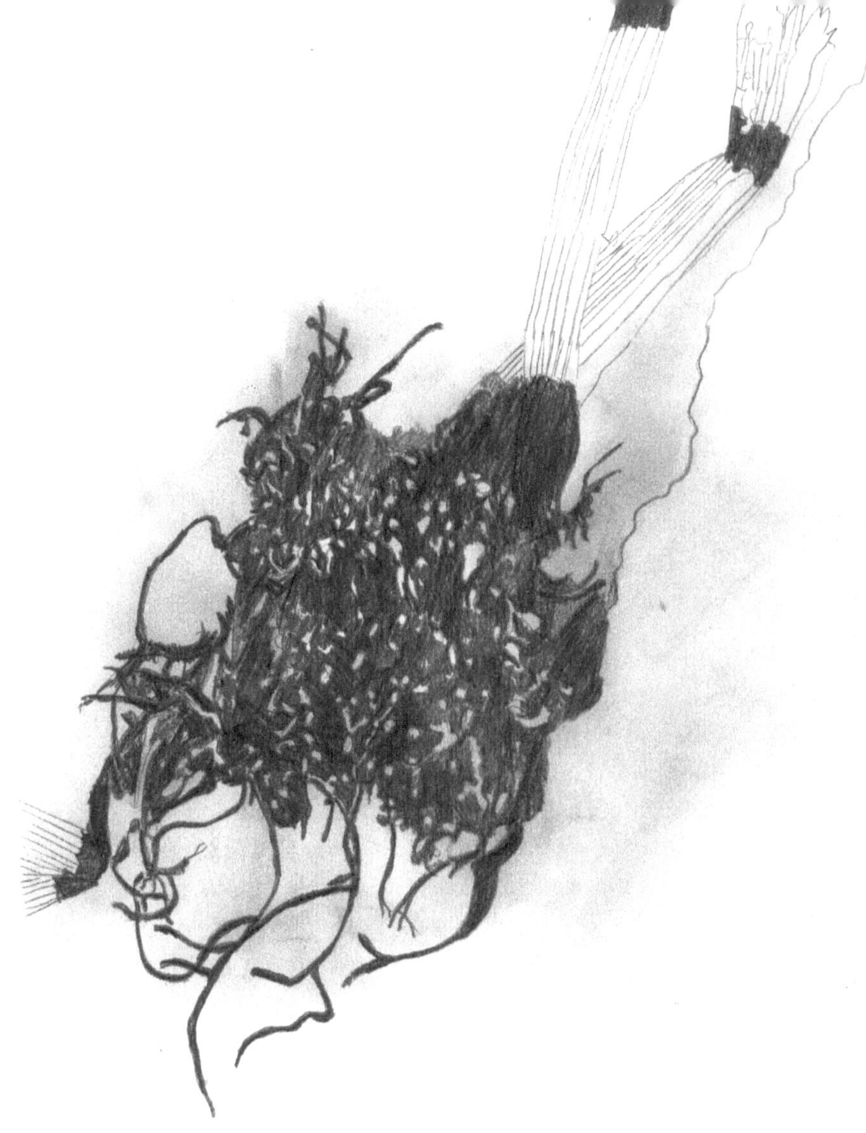

claustrophobia. It is not possible for more than one person to squeeze through the door. At its right-hand corner is a large heavy cupboard. There is a mirror inside, but when opened, the cupboard holds nothing and the mirror merely reflects the viewer's own face.

♦

Please Note.
It is possible to miss exhibit 167 on a first visit.

♦

The blankness of the hallway, the stained floor-boards, the darkness [there is no skylight] may cause the visitor to be initially disappointed. How does TRACe compete with the grand hallways of other museums with their chandeliers and their uniformed attendants? The answer is: it cannot do so. In a place such as this the viewer should ask no questions, but simply embrace the experience.

There are no guided tours. To the first-time visitor it might seem a place of nothingness. But revisit TRACe again, return with an open, curious mind and you will be rewarded. On an ordinary day, in winter perhaps, when the frost is back on the ground and there is a chill in the air, when the wind whips the entrance shut, you will experience something extraordinary. Or visit in the spring when cherry blossom carpets the ground, or on those summer days when even the strongest sun cannot penetrate the lacquered darkness of the hallway. In those moments of return, look closely and listen. Hark! Far away, above and beyond the sounds of planes passing overhead, the slow tread of feet on the pavement outside, the murmur of hushed voices, far away from the sounds of life continuing its flow, is another gentler sound. Follow it for a while as you walk down the hall, through to the other rooms, and you will hear a faint echo, a shadowed presence of a hundred years. Listen closely, dream a little, and the noises will grow stronger as you dream.

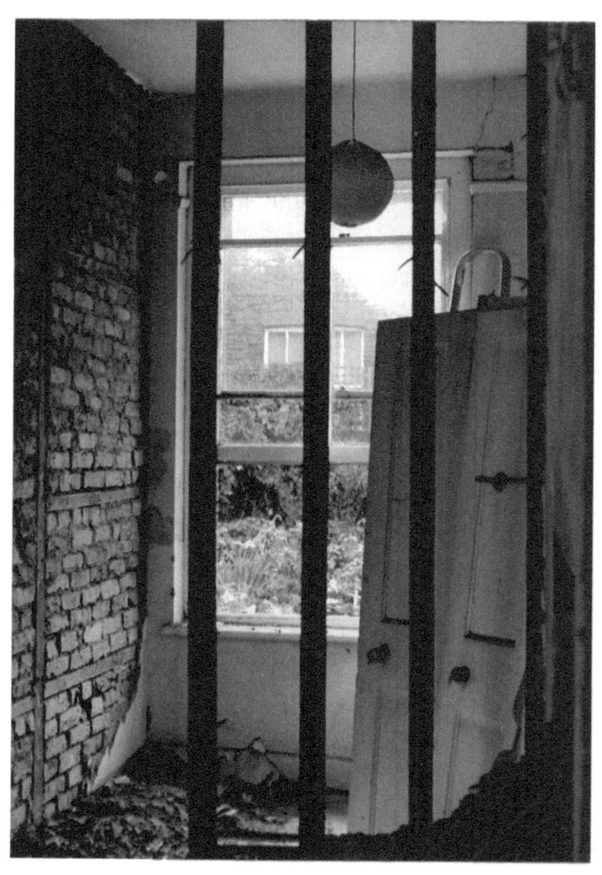

III

THE MASTER BEDROOM

In her dreams, Ursula would vividly recall her parents' bedroom. In her dreams, she stood just inside the doorway and remembered how she would steal a look at herself in the long mirror. How did she look? Her mother's mirror was usually sympathetic towards her appearance. Even young girls need sympathetic mirrors. The curse of appearance exists from the very beginning of time and so, Ursula liked looking at herself in her mother's looking glass. The mirror and Ursula were usually engaged in some sort of argument, even in her dreams.

The room is completely changed now, of course. It exists solely in Ursula's mind and sometimes she thinks it is clearer there, tucked away amongst the lost photographs.

♦

She likes to talk about it sometimes. This room and all it represents has a special place in her mind. This, after all, is the room where her mother died.

♦

Her mother gave Ursula her first bra in this room.

Her mother knelt on the floor of this room examining the green carpet looking for blonde hairs belonging to Ursula's father's mistress. Her mother drove Ursula mad in this room with her wailings and her despairing cries.

What was Ursula to do? She was only fourteen.

'Leave him,' she said with the full weight of youth's callousness.

'Where shall I go', her mother had cried, standing in this room, fear in her eyes.

Ursula had been busy glancing sideways at herself in the mirror at the time. Yes, she was thinking, I don't look so bad, after all. Not bad at all.

'Are you listening?', her mother had asked, or rather, shouted.

They had both caught a glimpse of themselves; the older woman and the young girl. One leading the other towards an unknown destiny.

Yes, Ursula had thought, I look quite nice, really.

What neither of them knew was that in twenty-four years and fourteen hours Ursula's mother would be dead.

In this room and on this bed with its mustard and dull green eiderdown.

The eiderdown that had been bought in Petticoat Lane, that popular haunt of sixties immigrants.

Let me tell you about that eiderdown. It is long gone now. It went along with Ursula's mother, following her into the unknown, becoming one of the earlier archival losses. By the time it had gone it had lost its satin shine. Just like Ursula's mother. And although Ursula had hated it then, afterwards she began to collect things that were mustard and green. You might say that love grew out of hate in this instance and not the other way round.

Yes, thought Ursula, on the day they had argued. I do look nice. She stood in front of the mirror twisting a strand of blonde hair.

◆

The room, wrongly labelled by the estate agent as the master bedroom, is now a shrine to Ursula's mother.

It is a place of empty chairs and unslept-on pillows.

A place where only silence reigns, waiting for the next human drama.

For a room that had once held the dead, however briefly, would always lie in wait to catch the guilty.

Two candles burn in this master bedroom. One green and one yellow. They represent all the years of the eiderdown's life.

◆

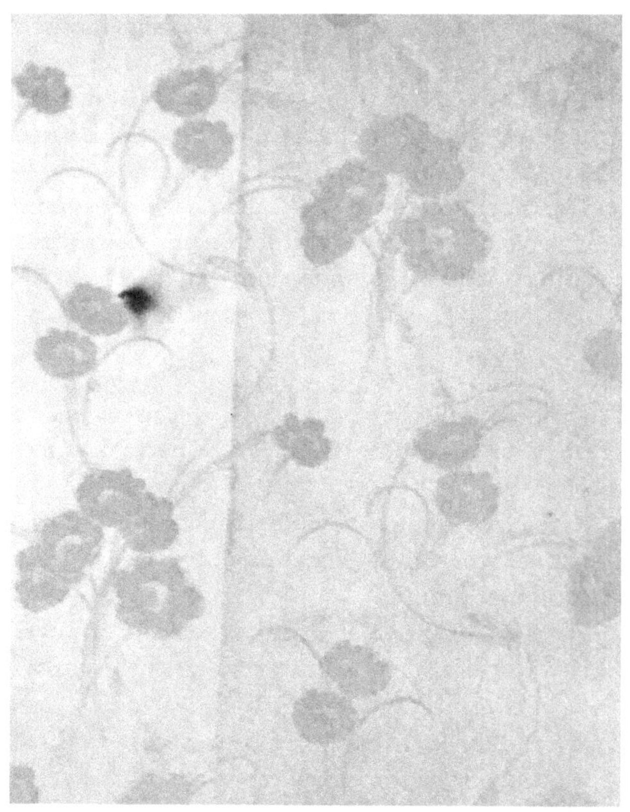

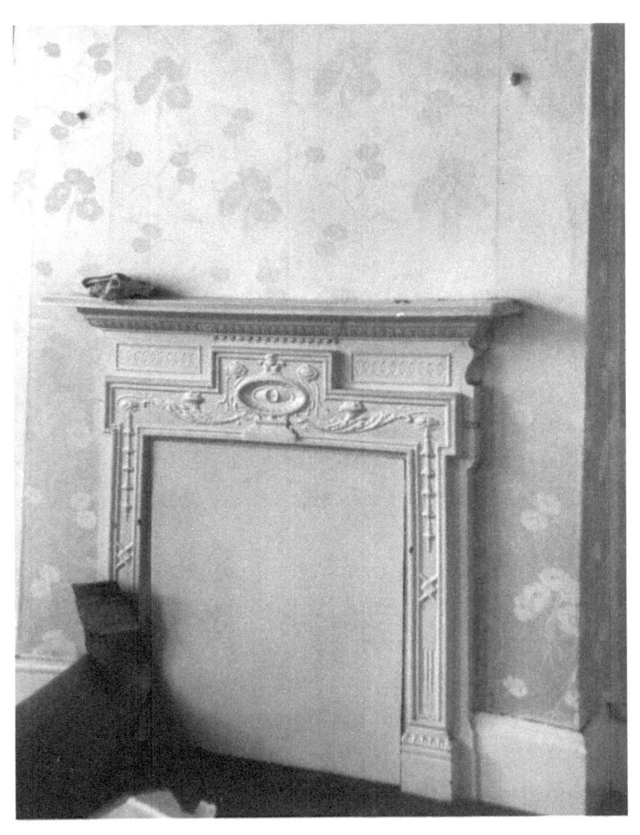

23

There are other things in the room, too.

A shoebox of dead things.

Another lock of hair of which Ursula once caught a glimpse before it was snapped shut. This hair was of a different colour.

An embroidered rosebud. How on earth could Ursula still remember it after only a passing glance?

Death lay in that room, Ursula realised. How could she not have realised it?

•

It is in this room that she had had chicken pox.

And told tall stories to both her parents.

Lies, all lies.

Ursula had grown used to lies by the time she was twelve [possibly younger].

It was a room where she was a child. But only just.

A token of this passing phase in her life still resides in the room now. It is there in the form of a height chart, tracking her progress through childhood. After a time, the pencil marks fizzled out through lack of interest. Or maybe it was simply that she stopped growing.

There is a mirror in the archives of this room now. After all, hadn't mirrors always played an important part in the life cycle of this room?

•

Aside from the shoe box, there are other mysterious traces from long ago.

The net curtains that Ursula remembered so clearly simply added to the gloom.

Sunlight never ventured into this waiting-room of death, this antechamber.

Evil lurked in a damp patch on the wall.

A patch that never went away.

Could death wait twenty-four years, wondered Ursula?

Was it really that patient?

Ursula had wanted low music and a red velvet curtain in this room.

She had wanted fact and fiction to enter its four walls with stealth.

She had wanted this story of memory and sadness told with hesitation and some uncertainty.

And she wanted a damp patch on the wall, just as she had remembered.

But we, the curators, denied her these requests.

◆

There is box marked FORBIDDEN in Ursula's second archive.

She had no idea what was in it. Best, she decided, to keep it that way.

If her memory served her correctly, Ursula had always known about the existence of that box, [quite different from the other shoebox] forever.

She had had only marginal curiosity about it

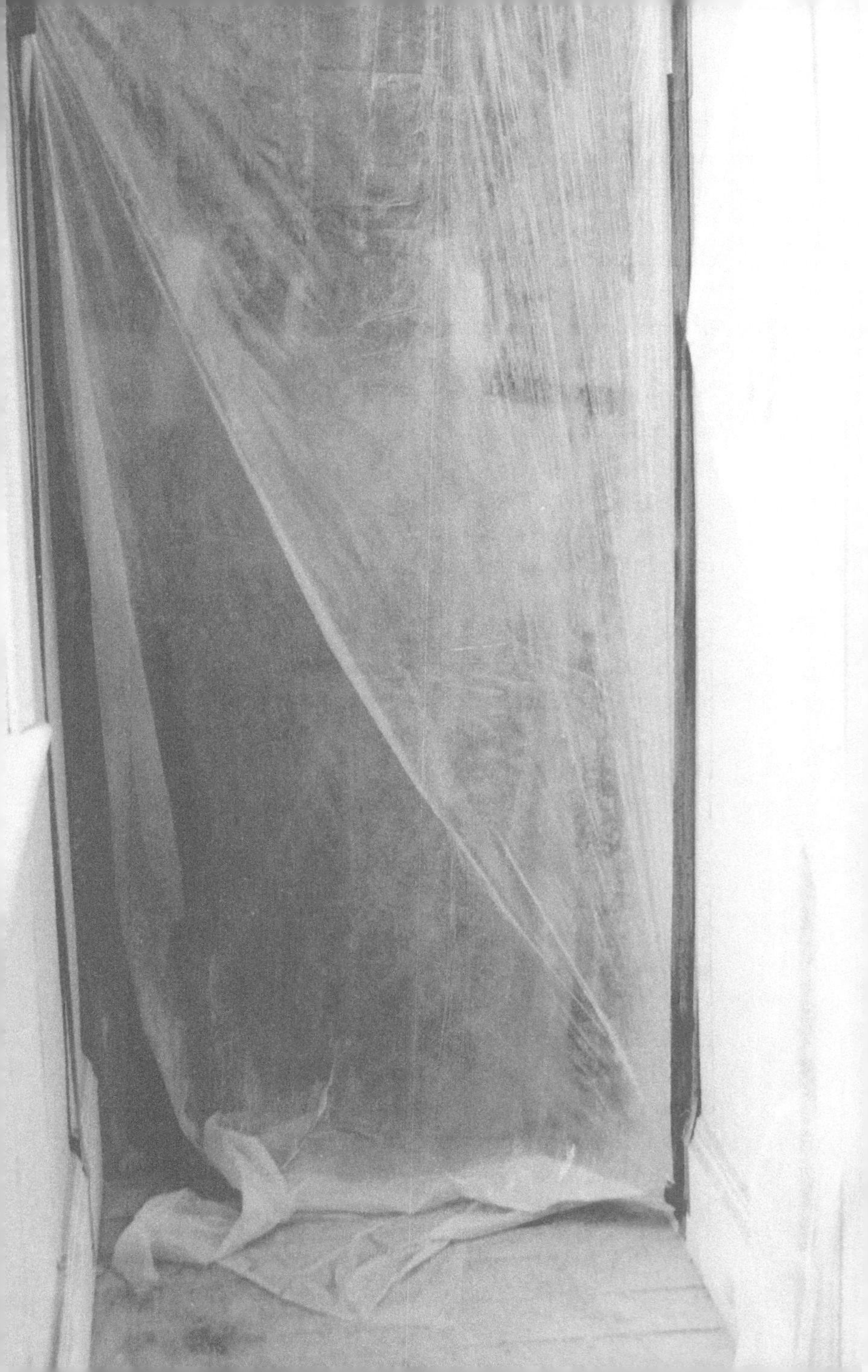

when she was growing up.

In those distant days there were so many forbidden things, why focus on the box marked forbidden?

But later she had acquired the itch of wanting-to-know.

Still, it was best left alone, she decided, when she was older. And she included it in the trunk donated to us.

◆

There used to be a photograph in this room arranged over the mantelpiece. A child once turned it to face the wall. Ursula's mother had screamed in terror when she saw what the child had done.

There would be a death soon, she had screamed.

No one knew that her look of terror was for herself.

Had she looked death in the eye?

The photograph was of Ursula's father.

He didn't die. Not then, at least.

But his photograph, for some mysterious reason, was in Ursula's small remaining collection. Still.

When we were given it, she had covered up the image with a black cloth. She refused to look at it, fearing that by looking she would evoke some dark and magic spell. Her father, after her mother's death, had communed with ghosts. So, though she was happy to include his photograph in her archive, she refused to allow its face to be seen.

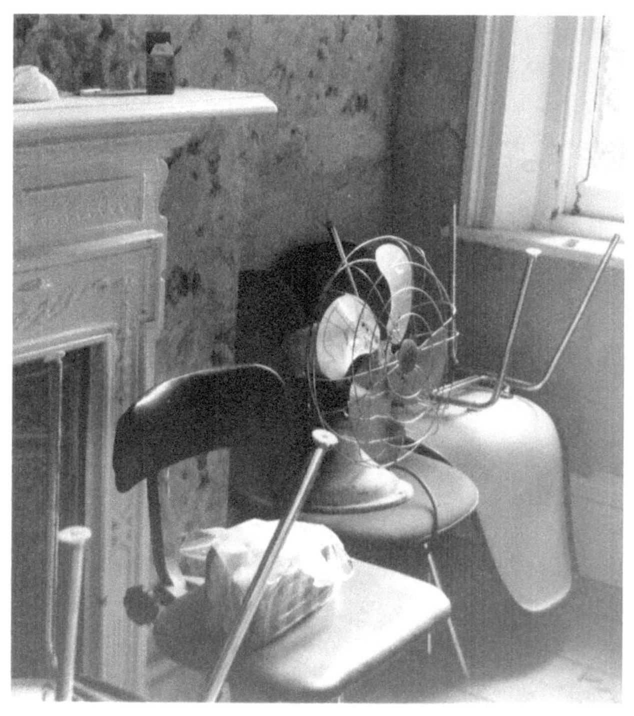

I V

THE SITTING ROOM

THE BOOKSHELF
During the entire 1960s, Ursula's mother's bookshelf was filled with books from her past life.

Some were as follows:
The Complete Works of Shakespeare. Gilt-edged, leather-bound. Inscribed with the initials N.M.C., this was the class prize for her First-Class degree in English.
The Palgrave Book of Twentieth-Century Poetry.
The Lotus Eaters. A Reader's Digest book club choice, author unknown. Dust jacket slightly torn. Some foxing on the endpapers.
One Way Street. Walter Benjamin. Unread. Pages pristine and uncut.
Happenings in a Museum. A textbook.
The Book of Disquiet. Fernando Pessoa.
The Emergence of Memory. Author unknown. Unread.
Two ebony elephants standing at either end of the bookshelf.

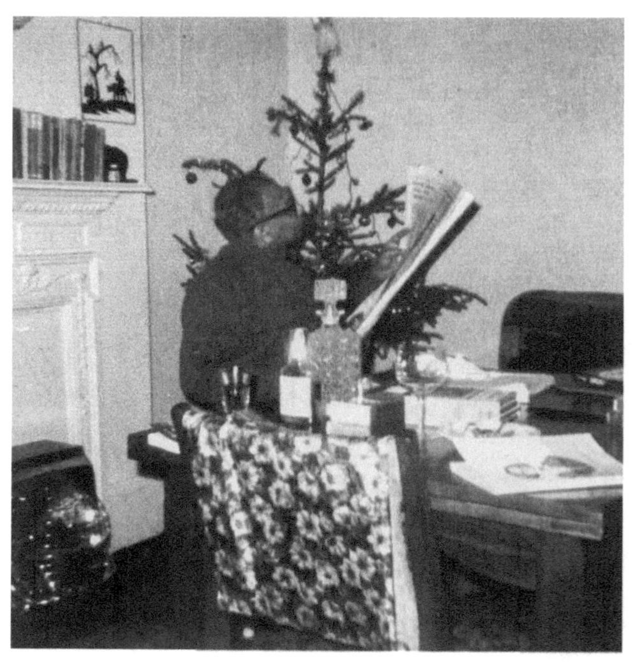

THE WALL

There was a quotation on the wall, written in minute handwriting:

Every day the material world mistreats me. 233 [52]. The writing had faded in the sunlight. Likewise, the spines of the books.

Also on the walls were two black metal pictures of a man carrying a basket of fish. Behind him was a stunted willow tree with no leaves. The trunk looked burnt. Perhaps it had been blasted in some fire. The whole effect was pretty desolate.

Ursula could not understand why anyone would make a tree with no leaves. She had lived with those pictures all her life. When they were lost, she began to see them more clearly with some sort of inner eye. She could no longer get rid of them.

Also on the wall were more dates marking Ursula's heights. According to these, she seemed to have stopped growing by the age of thirteen.

THE MANTELPIECE

The fireplace below the mantelpiece was of cast iron. It had been painted yellow. There were two blue vases on the mantelpiece that reminded Ursula of a painting she had once seen but whose name she could not now remember. Her mother had bought the vases from a stall in Coldharbour Lane. Her mother loved that name.

'A Cold Harbour,' she had exclaimed, 'how amazing!'

The name conjured up many conflicting memories for her.

She called it Cool Harbour Lane in memory of the cooling breeze that was forever present near the harbour wall. In their other home.

When she had noticed the blue vases in a stall, she had bought them both without hesitation. It had been an impulse-buy of course, but worth it for the images it conjured up. One day soon after her mother died, Ursula accidentally dropped one of the vases. It shattered, and the other one vanished in mysterious circumstances.

THE PHOTOGRAPH

One of the photographs in her mother's and subsequently Ursula's original collection had been taken on some Christmas Day a very long time ago. Ursula had no idea which year it was, but her father looked young and the Christmas tree they had been so proud of looked a little bare, in retrospect.

There was a table in the middle of the room. It was folded up to form a square and was, she later remembered, opened out only when guests came to lunch. The chairs they sat on in that room were covered in a fake-silk fabric patterned with white flowers. Ursula remembered her mother had covered what was the original even more hideous fabric with her awful fake-silk. Her mother was an excellent seamstress but had no eye for colour.

Also in that photograph were:

A bottle of whisky [her father drank whisky].

A cut-glass decanter [half full].

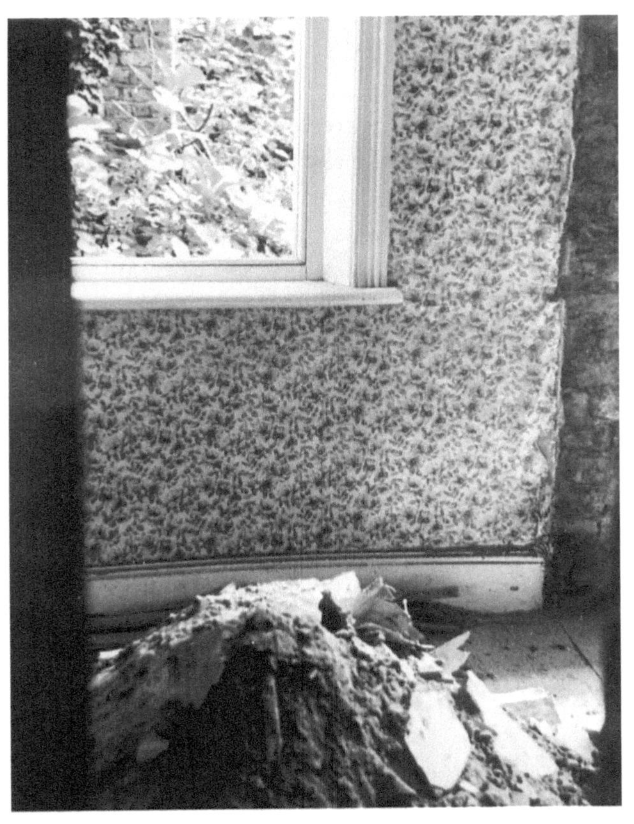

A box of chocolates.

Coles Notes on George Eliot's *Middlemarch*. [Ursula worked out that she would have been seventeen and about to take her exams when the photograph was taken].

A box of matches.

And a packet of cigarettes.

Nothing else was in the photograph.

WHAT WAS IN THE REST OF THE ROOM?
A sideboard that housed a set of gramophone records. These were:

Elgar's *Salut d'Amour*.

Overtures from some of Mozart's operas.

Beethoven's *5th Symphony* [Complete].

Beethoven's *Pastoral Symphony* [Complete].

Wagner's *Tannhäuser* [The Evening Star].

Tchaikovsky's *The Sleeping Beauty* [Overture].

Swan Lake [Complete. Russian version].

Despite this collection, Ursula's father played only one particular record over and over again.

♦

There were several plants on the sideboard, all extra-large begonias of a particular garish colour. Ursula's father was keen on garish colours. After a while, Ursula lost interest in bright colours and after her archive was destroyed, she began to use only traces of carmine and a watered-down blue. Mostly she loved anything that looked tea-stained or sepia. In accordance with her wishes, the museum has used only neutral colours. It is often possible to re-imagine the bright equatorial colours which filter though.

◆

The piano was the other item of furniture not visible in the photograph but living in the room. It was old, of unknown make. And it was nearly always out of tune. Ursula had loved it. For many years it had been her salvation as she was able to lose herself in the music. It disappeared after she left home in the same mysterious way other things belonging to her had vanished.

THE VANISHED:
ABRSM music grade books.
Years of theatre programmes.
Ballet shoes.
A large painting of a wheat field with crows in it. [Her art teacher had wondered why she had not painted her old home instead].
A stack of *Letts Schoolgirl's Diaries*.
Clothes that were too small for her but that she had wanted to keep.
Ursula's mother could be ruthless when she wanted.

◆

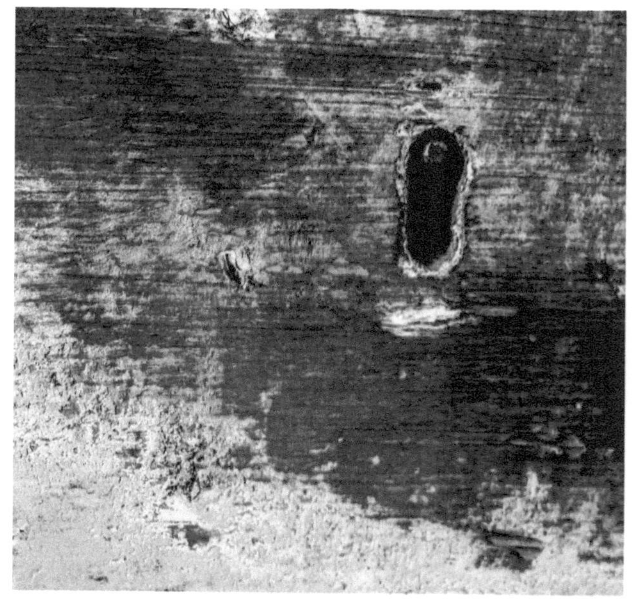

One last thing that had been in the original trunk that was gifted to us was a collection of scrap books from the 1930s. They had been thrown out by her mother and Ursula had wept over the loss. The magazines, from which her mother had carefully pasted all the things that had once interested her, could never be replaced.

Ursula had turned on her mother, and her mother, for her part, said she had no idea Ursula had wanted them.

'I looked at them all the time,' Ursula had shouted. 'You knew! You knew!'

But nothing remained, not the scrapbooks nor the conversation that had ensued. Only the sound of anger remained eternally present, living in the room that had once been a family room in which to relax. Soon this room itself would become a diluted shadow of its former self.

We at TRACe have preserved that anger for all to experience.

V

URSULA'S ROOM

Contained:

A mirror.

Some paper roses.

Ring-a-ring-a roses. [The pandemic was more than fifty years in the future so no worries there].

Green wallpaper. [Why do children keep all their old treasures? Why don't they discard them?]

A picture.

◆

In the picture there was a family of hedgehogs living inside a tree root.

Blue light and a warm stove.

Mother hedgehog wearing an apron.

The children, unlike lonely-only Ursula, were many. They sat around the table, waiting for food. Their faces glowed in the warmth of the kitchen.

Ursula wanted to belong to a family like that.

She wanted to live inside a tree.

Did her desire for a family grow from this one picture? Was it the image that informed her adult life?

A lot of the archives in that trunk were from her bedroom.

           •

There was a picture of the bed where the cat slept.

The windowsill where the ornaments [trinkets of no value] were kept. They were arranged just so.

No one dared move any of it. Not even Ursula. The rules were strict. Dust would gather before anything was moved.

'Why keep this rubbish?' her mother had asked.

But although she did not know it then, Ursula's 'rubbish' would one day be a precious memory.

'We all want to predict the future,' her mother had snapped. 'But we only catch shadows.'

Some images remain, others do not.

Why had the box with shells pasted all over it been saved when nothing else had?

Her mother had written a message on a scrap of paper. Ursula stole it and pasted it on her bedroom wall.

To be happy is to be aware of oneself. And to live without fright.

'Why have you taken my message?' her mother demanded, hiding her fear for Ursula's future life under the safety of anger.

Ursula did not know the answer, but a great sadness came over her.

She slid her painting, the large one now lost, of

the wheat field with a crow, behind her wardrobe. It would stay there for years. And then vanish. Somehow Ursula sensed even then, that this would happen.

◆

On the wall was a calendar with an image from the ballet, Les Sylphides.

A bad reproduction.

The year was 1965. One hundred and ten years since the painter Van Gogh had been born. Ursula kept the calendar without changing it for five more years. There seemed no point in replacing it.

She knew she would leave the house one day. So the calendar could stay as company for the vacated room. So she thought.

When she returned, she knew she would be a different person with a different mind-set.

What she didn't realise was that the room would have been changed. Ursula's mother would see to that, changing everything, beyond all recognition.

Why keep a nest when the bird has flown, she was heard saying.

Maybe, Ursula thought, folding up her rage, her mother might have adopted a different tone of voice? One that was more sympathetic, perhaps?

It might have helped. But of course, the old, she decided bitterly, are inflexible and lack understanding.

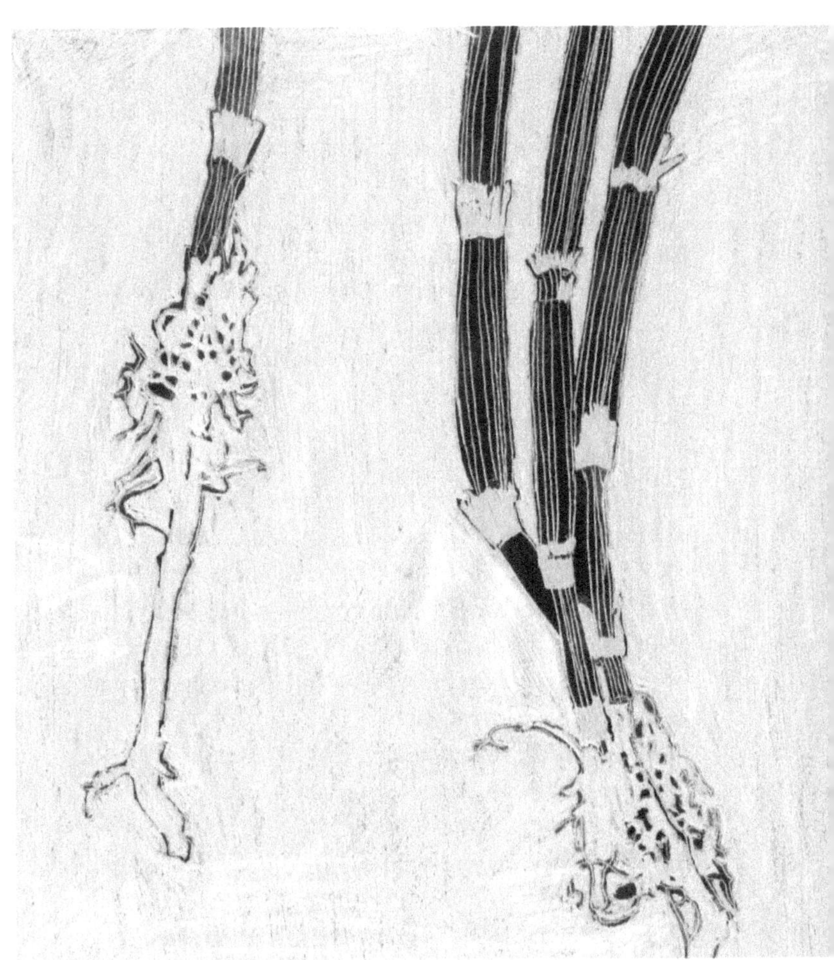

So, because of her mother's foresight [or was it malice?], Ursula was not shocked when she returned to retrieve her possessions and found them missing.

Everything had been thrown out in this room too. Nothing remained except some shards of memory.

'I need my memories', Louise Bourgeois had said. 'They are part of my documents.'

True, thought Ursula. And then she added, 'Lucky you, Louise!'

♦

In this room, Ursula's mother had removed all that was lime green and gentle and replaced it with mustard and khaki furnishings. Again. Had her mother become obsessed with army colours, Ursula wondered? Perhaps it simply served as a reminder that the war which was raging in their far-away home had been the real problem. Perhaps it was a reminder for her mother?

Ursula didn't need reminding about the war that had made them what they were.

'All refugees are obsessed by war,' her ghost mother told her, after she died.

'I'm not,' Ursula told the ghost.

'You!' Her mother's ghost said scornfully.

She didn't finish the sentence. Ghosts seldom do.

♦

Now the room belongs to our museum. It had been preparing for this eventuality for years, and somewhat belatedly Ursula realised this. The walls needed to be taken down and replaced with new ones. In this way it is hoped that the voices trapped inside will dissipate.

Of course, that won't happen.

Some things cannot be erased. Small things, softer than the sound of a mouse scuttling across floorboards, remain.

An adult crying at night. [Why did that sound so terrible?]

The habit of reading in bed.

A night light.

A dustbin being placed on the balcony in the next block of flats. [This was a sign for Ursula that the coast was clear for something clandestine that her mother knew nothing about.]

A sigh of pleasure during a moment of now-forgotten happiness.

The sound of a string of pearls being broken.

Ursula had always known pearls suited her. Why then had she discarded them?

Two pearls rolled under the bed and remained there forever.

A hairbrush; cheap, plastic, pink.

♦

When Ursula left the house on that first occasion, she took her brush with her. But then, seeing how tawdry it looked when she placed it in the wider world away from the green gloom of her bedroom, she threw it away in shame.

And kept the regret of the act instead.

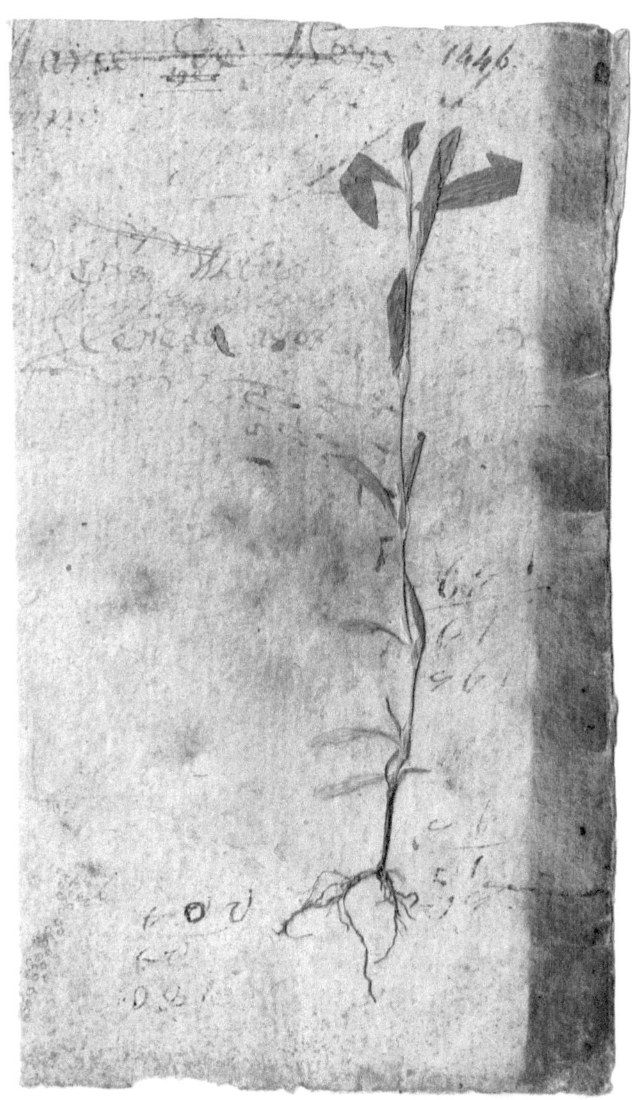

In her new life and while she was still young, her old green room shrank in impossible ways.

Or maybe she had simply grown? Whatever the answer, she found the room distasteful for some years after that.

During those years, those young, hopeful years, she was a bit like Orpheus. She promised herself never to look back. That, she realised later on, was a mistake. Never is a very long time.

Her friend Max, when he heard her say this, disagreed. He loved looking back.

'And look what happened to you,' Ursula retorted.

It was the only disagreement she ever had with Max.

                                                  ·

There was plenty of unhappiness in her bedroom. Maybe that was why children needed bedrooms? So they could play their unhappiness out in preparation for the adult world. But now, the problem was how to harvest these small miseries into the archive she had been forced to make to replace what had been lost.

Diaries helped, of course.

Year after year, ever hopeful, Ursula began a new diary that was never finished.

January 1st, she wrote.

Her father's birthday. A desolate day on which to be born.

None of her diaries remained.

Instead, these days, there are foxed papers with traces of past thoughts, hastily abandoned, scattered randomly across Ursula's mind.

Someone, probably Ursula herself, had drawn all over these traces in long trailing lines. Each line represented a voice. But what it actually meant was impossible to decipher.

◆

Some other things were left in Ursula's room.
Books, mostly black-covered
paperbacks, remained.
Black covers for foreign titles.
Zola
Tolstoy
Gogol
Chekhov
Dostoevsky
Flaubert

Had she really read all these?
And some cream paperbacks.
Hardy
Eliot
She couldn't remember the other names.

But by the time she left she had read them all.

No one, not even Ursula's mother, realised the significance of Ursula's leaving. But that day in September 1973 she shed the skin of yesterday as though she were a snake and left quietly.

No one noticed.

She was moving on. Yet they could not tell.

They were busy with their own misery, their fights, their refugee memories, other God-knows-what grievances. On and on it went, this useless re-living of their journey.

Ursula wanted none of it.

·

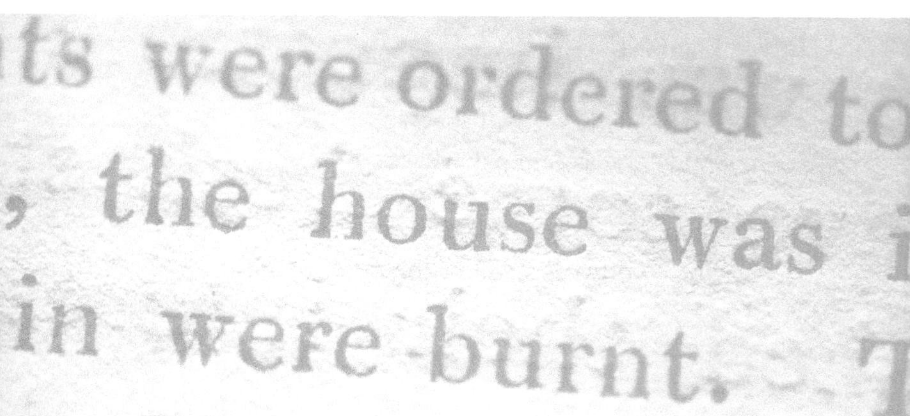

New life pushed against the walls of her bedroom demanding to be let in.

A jasmine creeper sprang to life.

When years later the room was destroyed to make a space for someone else's life, Ursula's memories were pushed aside. Or so she thought.

In fact, now that the room was floating freely, it was able to breathe.

It became a room inside another room.

A room that was green and golden and full of the distant horns of summers past.

A room that Ursula, returning with wiser, gentler eyes, liked best of all, because what was hidden there would remain this way.

Her friend Max disagreed. He did not believe in the hidden. To hide was to suppress all that mattered. He did not approve, he told her, bouncing his disapproval against the lost walls of Ursula's room. It had happened too many times in other places, he told her.

Maybe.

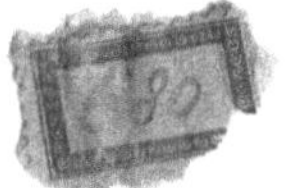

VI

THE KITCHEN

THERE WERE begonias on the windowsill grown there by Ursula's father. It was his contribution to the life of the kitchen. Naturally, these flowers too were red and yellow.

'Your father,' Ursula's mother used to say, 'has green fingers.'

She hadn't sounded that impressed.

Other remarks her mother made stayed trapped forever, in amongst the cooking scents within the kitchen. Sometimes these conversations floated out with the steam from the cooking water but mostly they stayed sealed within the bell jars that housed the sugar flowers.

Since Ursula had been born her mother had cooked 22,500 meals.

A lifetime of meals. All she wanted was a good kitchen but what she had was a narrow room with a window too high to reach.

Sometimes the sunlight came through but mostly this small space remained shrouded in gloom.

After her mother died, Ursula returned to stare

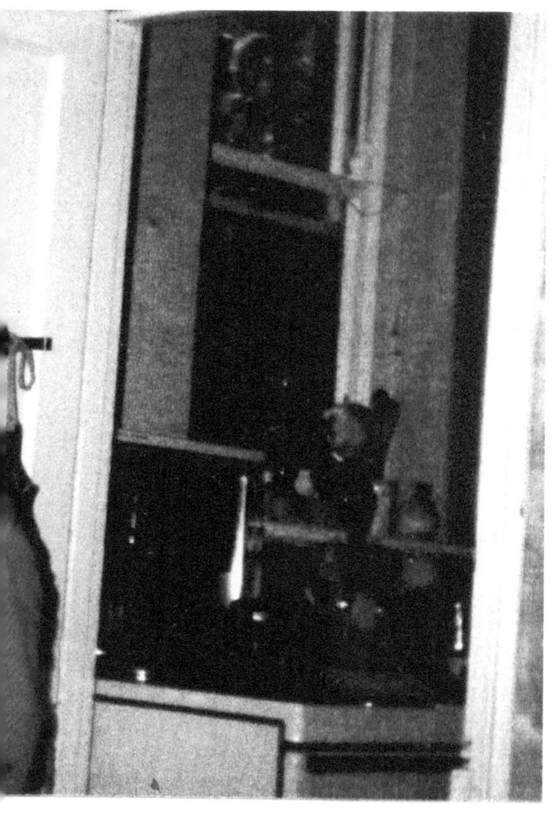

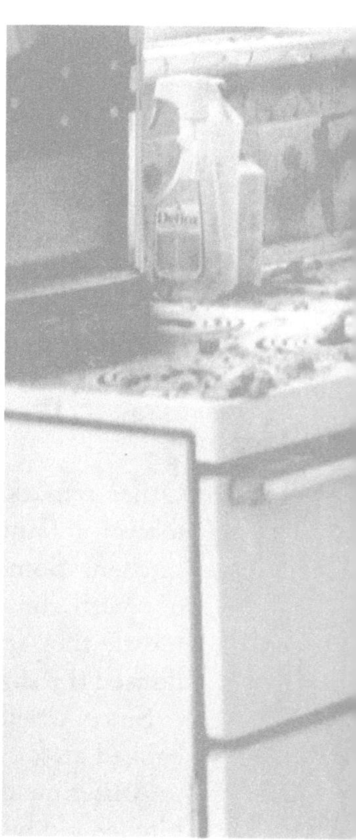

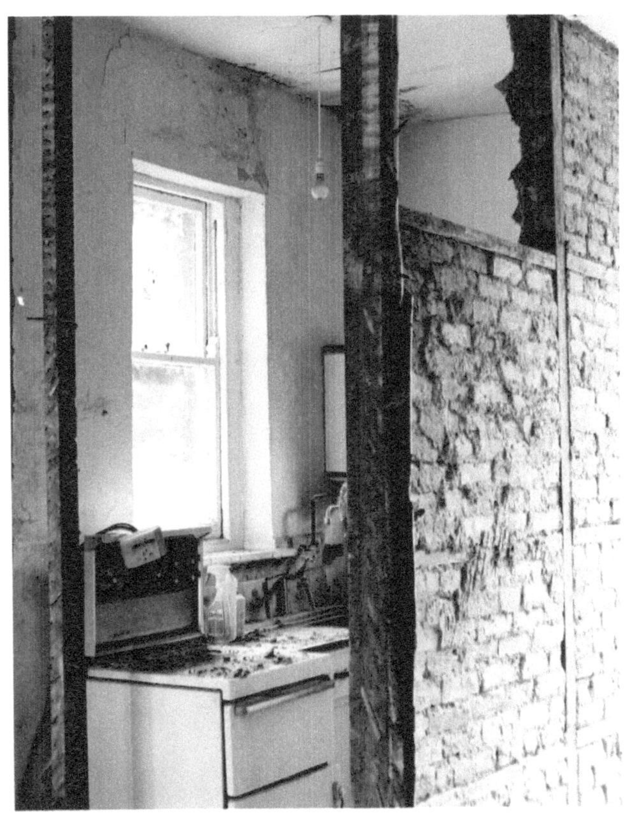

at the kitchen. She wondered if her mother had bought a new cooker but then realised that she had simply kept it clean for forty years. Her mother hadn't believed in upgrades.

The colours in that kitchen were still mustard and khaki. For heaven's sake! What was this obsession, Ursula wondered?

But now the old kitchen was gone and all that was left was the small high window that looked like a window to another era. Ursula paused seeing a cookery book.

It was battered, stained and foxed, just like an old man's hand.

Ursula wondered if her obsession with old papers came from this book.

These days her hands were beginning to look a lot like her mother's. And when she played the piano, she saw that there were cracks in her skin.

Ursula's mother had never played a piano.

Some things were different.

◆

Ursula had several questions that no one would ever answer.

She wondered about the very last meal that was cooked in this kitchen.

Did her mother eat alone?

Could it be that after all those years of feeding

others she had to eat her last meal without a single person in the room?

Her mother's foolishness had led to this loneliness on the last evening of her life. Her father, Ursula was certain, had been elsewhere. He was a man who did not appreciate what he had until it was lost.

In her solitary place at the table, wearing a headscarf to stop her from feeling the September cold, Ursula's mother would have thought about things no one would ever know. Her thoughts then locked themselves into the walls as though into a safe. Ursula knew she would never get the combination code.

◆

It was a loss like no other.

But what did she eat? Ursula kept asking herself.

Nothing of importance and everything of importance.

And then again, what had Ursula eaten on that last night of her mother's life? That too had been forgotten. Although her hastily-scribbled note to herself read: watched Curlew River. Very bleak.

Which is why we play the music from that opera throughout TRACe.

What is forgotten grows in importance.

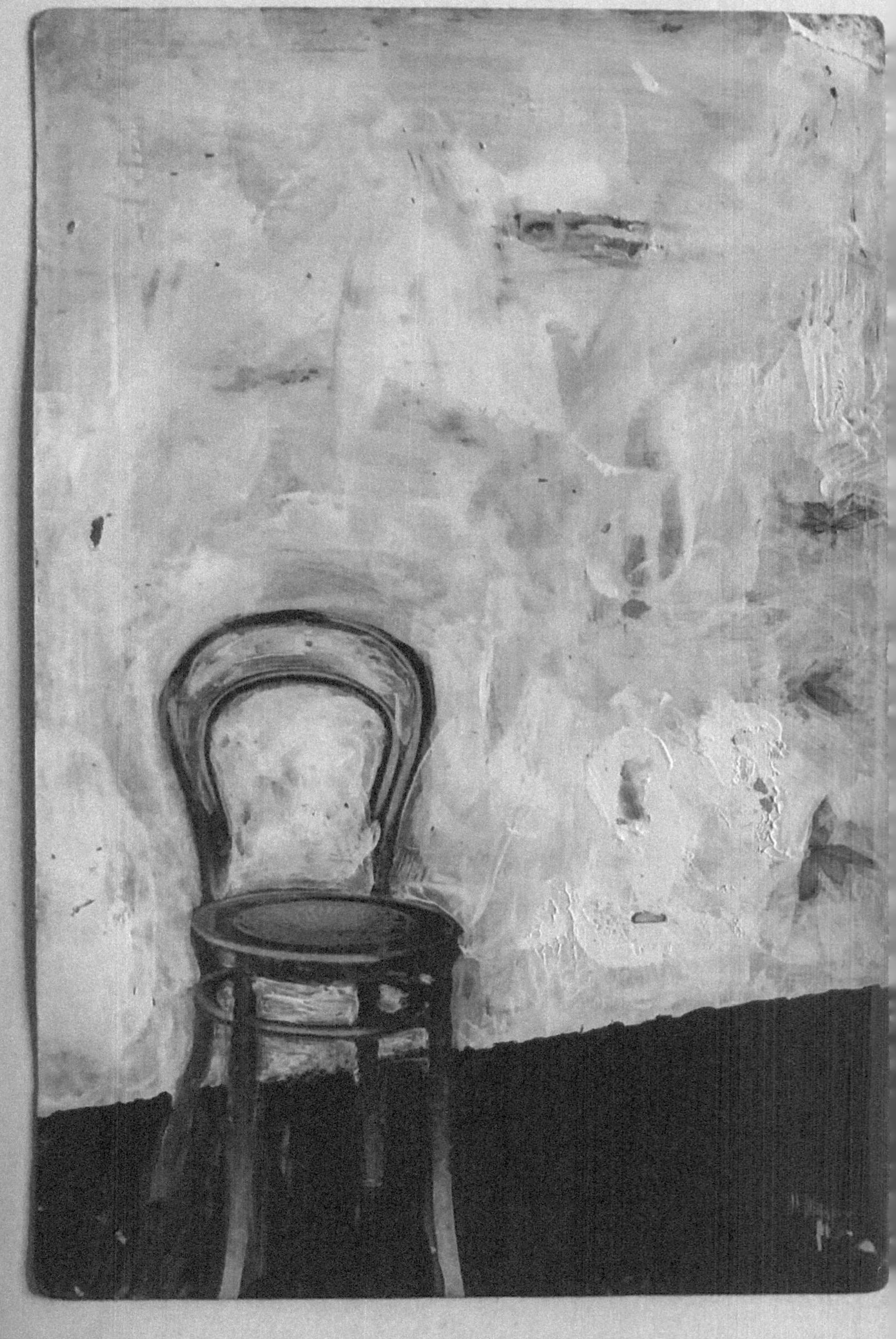

There had been two plates on the table and a saucepan of rice.

The mystery of that last meal remained.

'I will never forget,' Ursula's father said, 'the smell
of cooked food.'

He was lying; he forgot.

All the cutlery had gone.

The saucepans, the spice jars.

Ursula cursed the people who had taken them.

Only her mother's touch remained, like invisible
handprints on what had been vaporised.

No wonder Ursula's father could not live in that
house afterwards.

Ghosts followed him around like dogs, snapping
at his ankles. So, all he could do was flee as they
had once fled from their first home.

Thus was her father a refugee twice removed.

In the newly-decorated room that used to be the
kitchen, we, the curators, placed some empty jars
of spice around. If you prised open their lids, the
scent of a spice mill from their distant life rose up
and floated towards the ceiling.

We filled a few old jars with water, as instructed

by Ursula. Then we pasted the face of her mother onto each of them. The water distorted her mother's face so that it looked stretched in pain. Her mother's eyes stared out across the water as though waiting to be rescued. In the end, Ursula decided it was too much and demanded we fill the room with music. Her mother had gone. What was the purpose of trying to bring her back?

We, the curators, agreed.

◆

Next Ursula wanted to cook a meal so the vapour trail of scents would remain permanently in the space.

But of course, now there was no cooker.

And the noisy extractor fan had been dismantled.

So, there was nothing more to do in this part of the museum.

Still, returning with the questioning gaze of the adult orphan, Ursula saw many things – most of them beyond speech. It was best to have a silent archive in this space, she agreed.

She sighed. It was now, she felt, about the past of others.

✦

Once the cooker had been removed, we found the
skeleton of a dead mouse behind it. It must have
died forty years before.

Did old ghosts, even of mice, return?

✦

In the metal cupboard where her mother had kept
the few saucepans she possessed, there was a piece
of paper pasted to the door. It listed all the ingredi-
ents in the spice jars:

Cumin
Coriander
Chilli power
Cardamom powder
Fresh green chillies
Cloves
Coconut
Dried curry leaves
Semolina
Cornflour

✦

Dust collected in what had once been a dust-free environment.

The dust of all her mother's thoughts.

And some of her father's too.

Dust echoes everywhere, rising above the sound of the music.

It was how she concentrated all her lost archives into one single piece. Later on, others would collect dust as she did, but for the moment all dust belonged to Ursula alone.

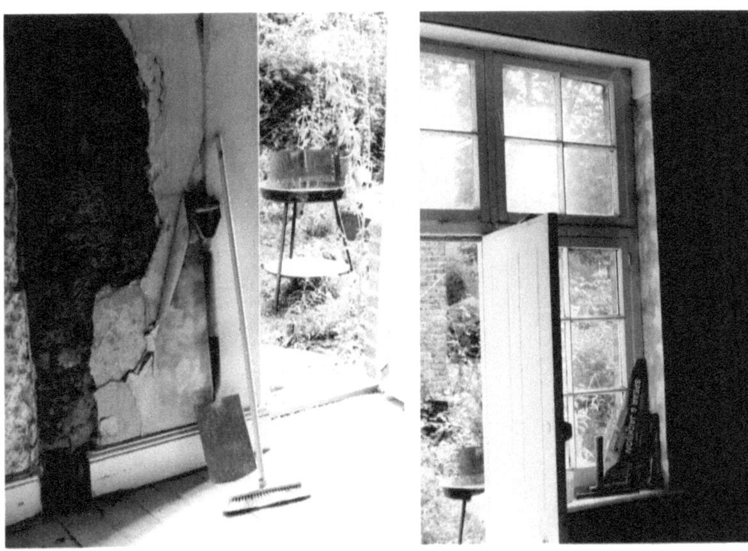

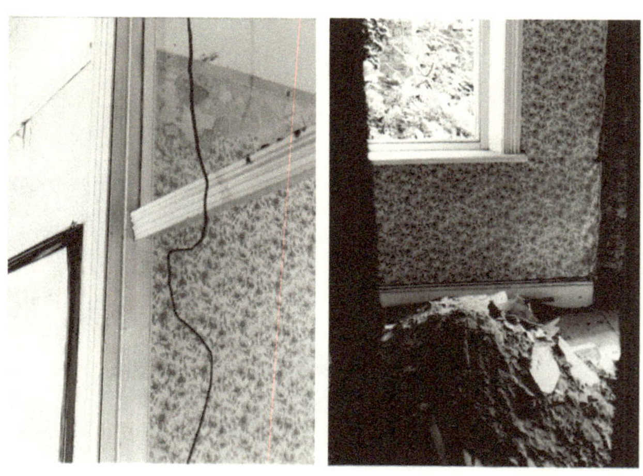

VII

THE BACK GARDEN

THE GARDEN is set on a piece of land so large one could build a housing estate on it.

It is large enough to create a market garden that sustains several restaurants.

Ursula's father was the gardener.

He grew:
A fig tree.
A plum tree.
Mulberry bushes.
A circle of roses.
And close-to-the-ground vegetables like cucumbers and courgettes.

Ursula hated her father's roses. It took years before she realised it wasn't roses she hated but the colours that her father loved so much.

Down the road in a little white house that Ursula longed to live in were pink roses and bluebells in spring. But Ursula's father was hooked on the colours red and yellow.

He had a poster of Van Gogh's sunflowers hanging on the wall.

The yellow reminded Ursula's father of home, he said, and although Ursula's mother used to have good taste [in Ursula's opinion] before they had become refugees, she too now loved everything that was red and yellow.

And so, the begonias continued to grow, as did the gladioli, and the bright, scentless roses.

Home called out brightly to them in paintbox colours.

Home was a Van Gogh sunflower, a curtain the colour of army uniforms, and the insides of pawpaw fruit.

The garden continued to grow. The damp patch caused by the drains remained damp, but the ginger cat rolled around in it when the sun shone.

In the summer, Ursula's father would bring in armfuls of figs and plums. Ursula's mother only knew how to make chutney with such unfamiliar fruit.

Not jams.

No one ate the chutney, and it piled up year after year along the top of the windowsill.

1965

1966

1967

1968

1969

When the new decade started, she stopped making it.

Ursula had flown the nest by then and begun a

secret life of her own.

She had given her parents everything she had and now wanted something for herself. If they were hurt, she did not care to notice.

'You win some, you lose some,' her father was reported as saying.

And he gave up on the garden.

Leaving her mother to just cry.

But the garden kept on growing like a fingernail on a corpse. And, in its own mysterious way, continued to flourish. Plums fell onto the grass, figs thudded on the ground and were attacked by wasps, courgettes grew to giant proportions and became marrows. And the roses continued to bloom. When asked, Ursula's mother said that pruning was a matter of personal preference. No one brought any of the vegetables into the house now, and the clothesline that had once held so many small wet things was bare as an espadrille tree in winter.

✦

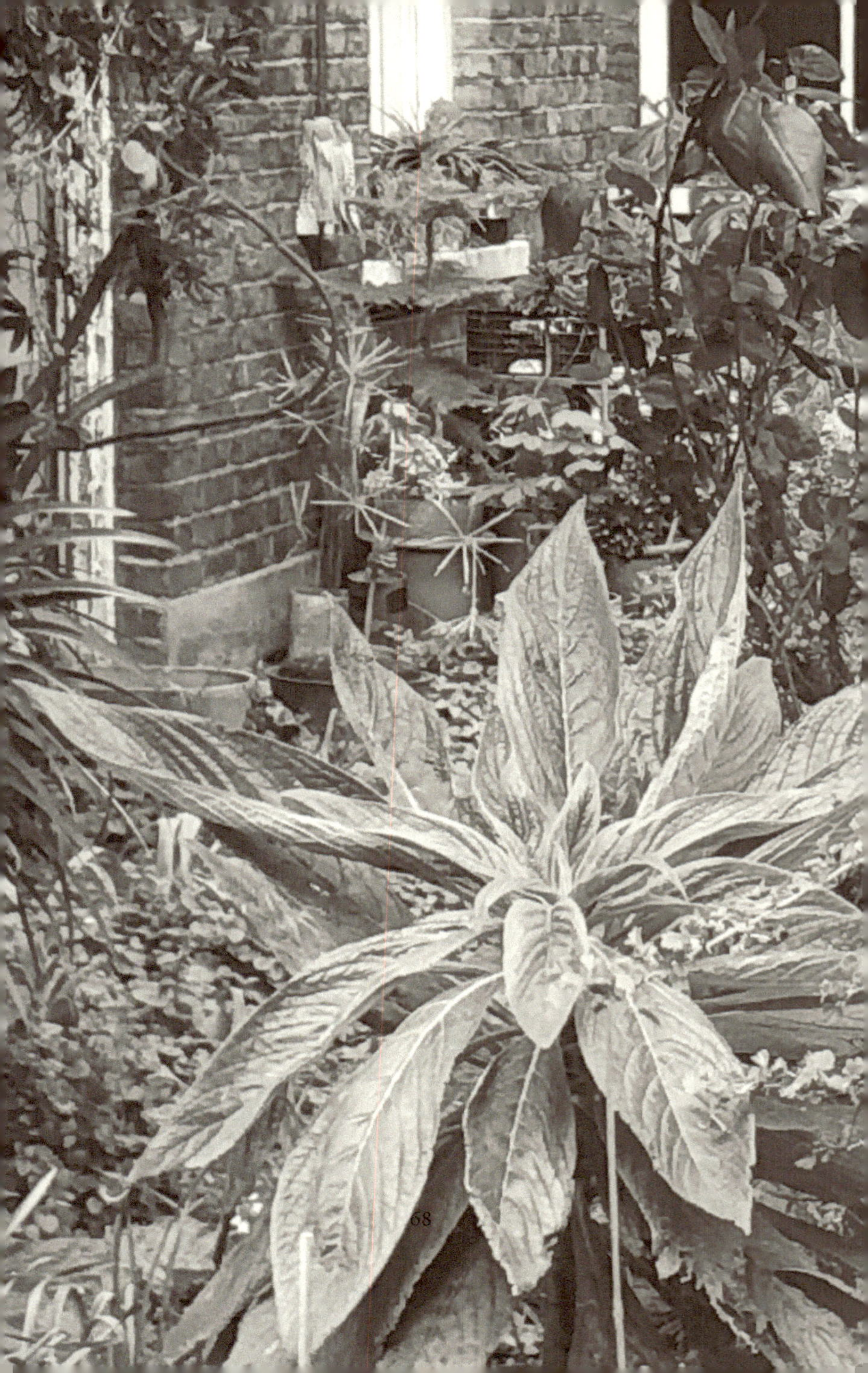

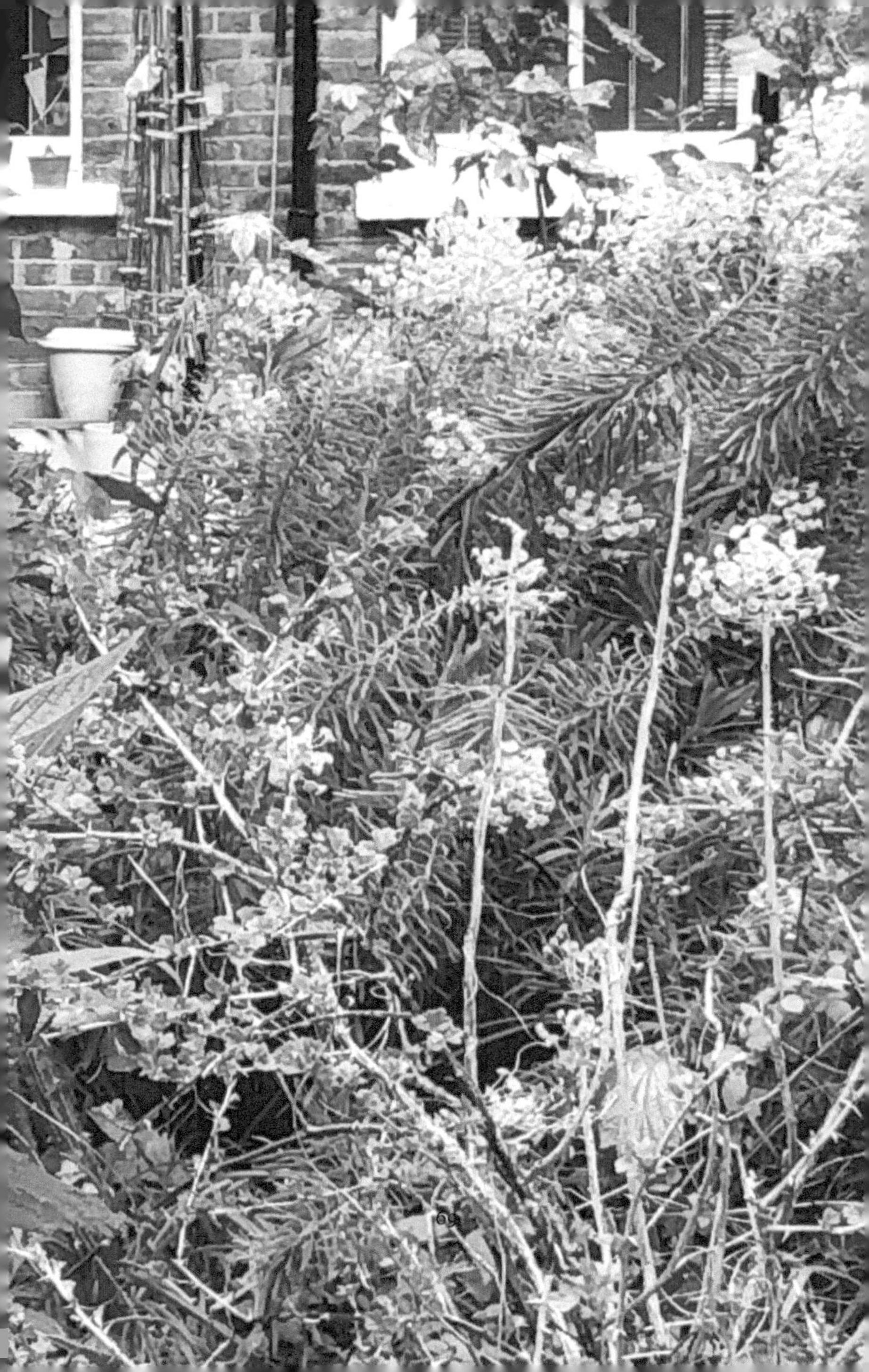

When the house was sold the garden revived
a little. Ursula found two bright yellow socks,
and these were hung out on the line where they
remained, fading slowly in the summer sun.

These were her garden archives.

Sunflower socks, she called them.

And when a crow perched on them one day, she
took a picture with her smartphone. The photograph reminded her of the inside of a tropical fruit
[she could not recall its name] that she used to eat.

Yellow with black seeds.

Some other garden memories survived too. By
now, Ursula thought fondly of yellow roses.
Proving that habit changes people.

So with this in mind, she packed a box of old
plastic roses into her archival trunk. They would
soon be planted in stiff rows in the garden, making
them look like flowers on a grave.

There were no ghosts present at that time, but
a stone with the dates 1920-1994 was written on it.

It would do, she told her old friend Max who,
although he did not know it, had himself only six
more years of life left.

·

The garden is the last place to be visited on this
tour of TRACe. To begin at the end is unrealistic.
No man or beast knows the end of any story. Now
the garden is littered with invisible graves. They

reveal themselves only if one looks through the long grass. Then certain things come to light.

A satin ribbon. Only Ursula knows why it is here.

'You don't need to tell us,' Max told her.

An old shoe.

'Any interpretation can be put on this,' Max said.

A seagull's feather.

A watering can so old its original colour had faded completely.

A label that said 'Victoria Plum. Brixton Beach Nursery.'

There were other things too numerous to mention but mostly what was important was the whispering breeze. The breeze talked to anyone who cared to listen. It talked about all that had gone on in the garden. It talked of those last summer days when Ursula's mother had sat alone with the back door open taking in the warmth of a September sun. She would not be needing the sun for much longer and her loneliness [Ursula's father was with his mistress] would not last for much longer either.

◆

After she died, Ursula's father came to stare at the garden. Regret lined the overgrown path. Guilt hovered in the red and yellow dahlias all ablaze with the oncoming autumn. There were sunflowers bowing as though in thought. A chair that had been placed by Ursula's mother on her last day of sunshine remained rusting in the autumn air. Had she forgotten to take it inside when evening fell? After her death, Ursula's father sat on it for a moment and felt his wife's shadow slip through him.

Ursula too would sit on that chair, but she had felt nothing. Not even guilt.

When the chair disappeared, she went in search of another and, as luck would have it, she found one exactly like it. She tied it to her overloaded trunk and dragged it around for years. Now it was back, placed by the garden door, waiting for the sunshine to return.

'What a piece of luck,' her friend Max said, sitting down, filling the absence by his presence.

Her mother, Ursula knew, would have been em-barrassed by the presence of such a famous man at her back door.

'I am not well known yet,' Max laughed. 'There are six more years to go. And then I will become a cult figure.'

He liked the asymmetry of his thoughts.

This, then, is the museum garden. It is the end of the trail that meanders through Ursula's archive. What is left is a walk through the streets where they had all, for such a brief time, once lived.

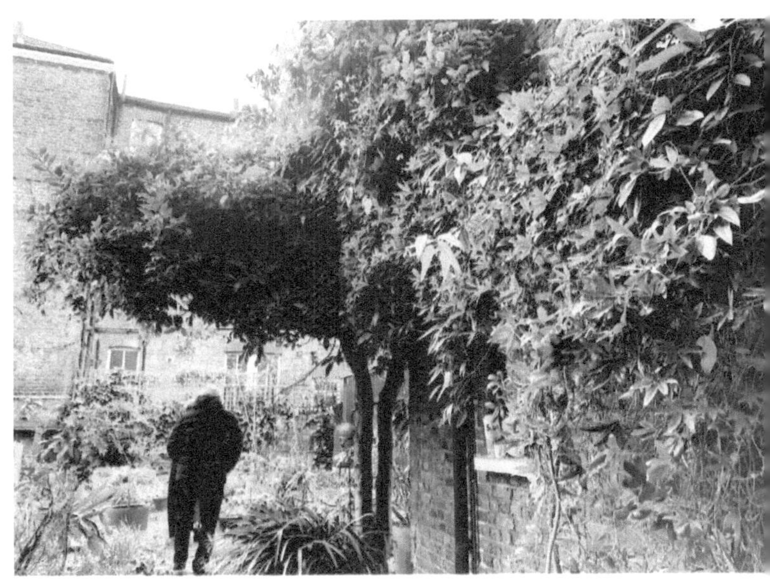

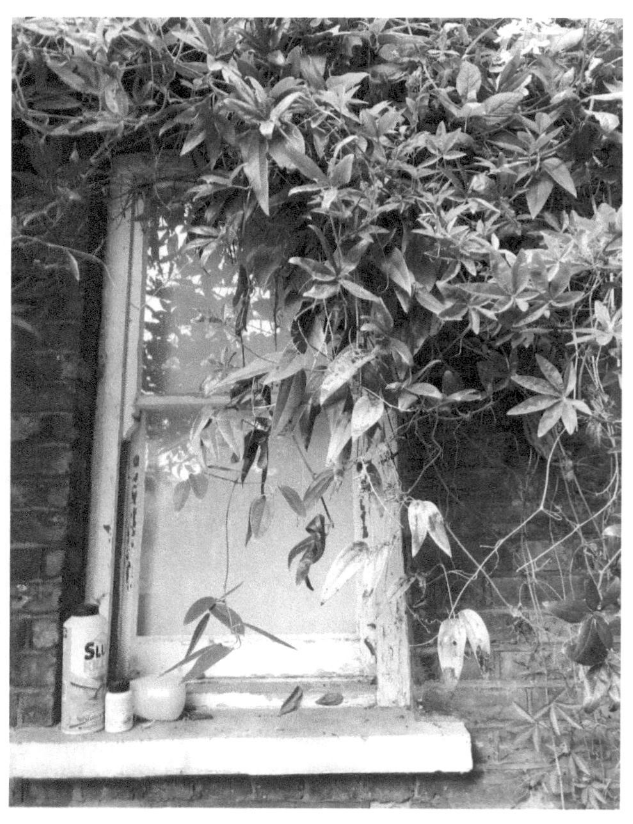

SOME NOTES ON THE BACKGROUND TO THE TRACe ARCHIVES

THIS ARCHIVE found its way to TRACe in a most unusual way. It had been March and I was waiting for the Van Gogh Café to open. A sharp, bitter breeze cut the air like a knife.

The woman waiting next to me shivered and drew her coat closer. Snow, she said out loud, was forecast for later. I nodded and then the door to the cafe opened and we went in.

Inside, fairy lights wound up a cast iron spiral staircase and plants hung down from the ceiling. We stood waiting to be served and as the steam from the coffee machine rose noisily into the air, the woman turned to me.

'You are not from round here, are you?'

I told her that I was in the process of buying a small flat nearby and she nodded. She had, she said, been living in this area for a very long time; forty years, in fact. She was, she added, the child of a war survivor.

'So, I'm carrying inherited trauma.'

I nodded. The café was almost empty and by some unspoken but mutual consent we sat down together at a nearby table.

She was looking, the woman told me, for the dead. Her mother being one of them. For the dead were not really absent. Close observation revealed that their history was only barely concealed beneath the surface of things.

'They walk these streets,' she told me. 'Following us around. Forever exiles.'

'These streets?' I asked.

'For me it happens to be these streets,' she said. 'For you it might be in other places; places that are specific to you.'

The conversations went on around her all the time, she said. Annoyingly. Interfering with new thoughts she might have. The dead, she told me, were noisy, unruly, and often very rude.

We drank our coffee in silence.

'This place was my home for ten years,' she said, querulously. And then she gave me the plastic bag she had been carrying.

'I think you should have it.'

She'd been carrying it around with her for years and each year what was in it had grown heavier. She had, she told me, grown weary with all that was in it and had been looking for somewhere to lay it to rest. She fixed me with a stare.

'You'll do. Keep it in your new house. Look after it. There will be more if you are interested.'

I protested that the flat I was buying was small and I had enough junk of my own to fill it with, but she would have none of it, insisting instead that I take it away and look through the documents.

'You are an artist,' she said. 'Artists need materials, don't they?'

'I am a poet,' I told her.

She nodded. And then she told me her name.

'Ursula,' she said. 'I was once loved by too many.'

It seemed a little far-fetched, but I didn't argue.

'There's lots more,' she warned, with a laugh. 'A trunk load!'

I wasn't sure I wanted any of it, but I took the bag home thinking I would throw it in the bin.

But when I got home there was a voicemail telling me my offer had been accepted and the flat was mine if I wanted it. I promptly put Ursula's bag down in the hall and in my excitement forgot about it for a few days. The next few weeks were busy. My house was still unsold, as the buyers were being held up by their own buyers. I didn't want to lose the new apartment. The estate agent, nervous for the sale to be concluded, wondered if I could get a bridging loan, if there was any way I could at least secure the place with a deposit. I did not want to do this, but then, after much deliberation, I decided to use my savings for the deposit, knowing that I might lose all of it if my own house sale did not go through. There followed a tense few weeks. The flat was in theory mine but I had still not sold my old house.

◆

One night, tired of thinking of the risk I was taking, I caught sight of Ursula's carrier bag. I had forgotten all about it and so, to take my mind off the tricky balancing act over the house, I decided to look through it. With only marginal interest I tipped the contents onto the living room carpet. What I found astonished me.

A small scrap of grubby paper, crushed under the weight of all that was in the bag, caught my eye. Someone had written in a barely distinct hand:

'Here we have a man whose job it is to gather the day's refuse in the capital. Everything that the big city has thrown away, everything it has scorned, everything it has crushed underfoot, he catalogues and collects. Ragpicker and poet: both are concerned with refuse.'

I stared at the mountain of ephemera that had been in the bag and knew in an instant that I needed to find Ursula again. To understand both why she had entrusted all of this to a stranger, and what on earth had her hoard it in the first place.

The problem was that I didn't know how to find her. I had asked for her phone number twice during our conversation and she had ignored me. Instead, she had put my number in her phone. Now I would have to wait for her to call me. If she ever would.

The material in my possession seemed random and a little pointless. Endless scraps of paper with lists written out in a painstaking manner. None of them related to each other.

⁕

What for example was the purpose of this list?

Dust from a pair of faded shoes left out in the sun for years.

Dust from the rose garden in the village of Lidice, destroyed by the Nazis in 1942.

Dust from the newspapers shredded in Fleet Street on the 12th of September 2001.

Masonry dust from the bomb crater at Ali Benabi Talibi on the perimeter of Baghdad on the 23rd of March 2003.

Dust on a saucepan found after an earthquake in 2018 in Italy.

Dust preserved from the logging of trees in the Amazon.

There were about three hundred such entries. And on another scrap of paper was written:

See here is my current forest dust collection. Pollen is a dust and lasts for thousands of years allowing extinct plants to be catalogued. And many years later, allowing extinct plants to return.
Pollen dust. Three sorts.
Leaf rot dust. [Oak].
Leaf rot dust. Two jars. [Ash and Beech].
Pine needle dust.
Soot and smoke from burnt diseased trees.

These were all dated 1845–2020.
I shook my head.
'So much dust,' she had written, ' has made me fearless. It made mortality less frightening, for dust has caked my life.'
And beneath this, in the same spidery writing of the earlier quotation:

'My past and your past are filled with the dust from our collective mistakes. Against the cultural poverty of our times, it feels right to examine this dust.'
I stared at the words. For whom were they meant?
And as I was puzzling over these, two things happened. The survey for the apartment I was buy-ing came through, and Ursula phoned.

'Well,' she said without preamble, 'I knew you would like them.'

Taken aback and a little annoyed I asked her how she knew whether I liked … [I paused, trying to think of a polite way of continuing] … the material she had foisted on me.

'Well,' she said again, 'I am about to give you a trunk load more.'

Oh really, I thought, irritated, what made her think I wanted any more of her scraps?

'You will then have Britain's largest collection of private memories,' she said. 'It's an extraordinary range of objects, recorded voices and memorabilia that link past to present times. You'll see.'

She made it sound as though she were doing me a favour. I frowned.

'Look,' I began, 'I'm in the process of …'

'Buying a flat,' she interrupted. 'Yes, I know. You can house the collection in there.'

'I'm sorry,' I said annoyed. 'I'm buying to let. There will be tenants there. It isn't a place to house your archive.'

She mumbled something.

'What?' I asked, wondering if I should put the phone down and be done with it. Really, I wished I had never set eyes on the woman.

'Wait until you see the things in my trunk. And in any case, as the apartment once belonged to my family, it would be good to return all the objects to their original resting place.'

And then she hung up on me.

They were in a mess, but nothing is more seductive for an archivist than the thought of taming unclassified material. Nothing is more absorbing to the Keeper of long-ago secrets than nosing through invisible stories that lie hidden in them. I, Emile Charpentier, mathematician, and intermittent composer, working in the field of randomness in our intimate lives was, the minute that trunk was opened, immediately hooked. Like all historians, and yes, I class myself as a historian too, I am possessed with a passion, an absolute nostalgia for origins. Origins that have no formal existence. During my research into the nature of Randomness I moved backwards to a point of departure until I eventually arrived at a place where beginning and ending coincided. When this first happened, I was startled into silence. I had been moving towards this place for so long that, having finally got there, I had no idea where to go next. Such is the nature of aspiration that it leaves one exhausted once the goal is attained. Or so it seemed to Ursula and now me, collector of Randomness and Disjointed Narratives. Worn out by this search for origins, faced only by absences and the spaces they occupied, I began to see the potential of what once was but now was no more.

I had my own story to tell of course, some parts of which were linear and some of which were obviously random. I could have, had I wished, described my life in London where I had lived and was rejected

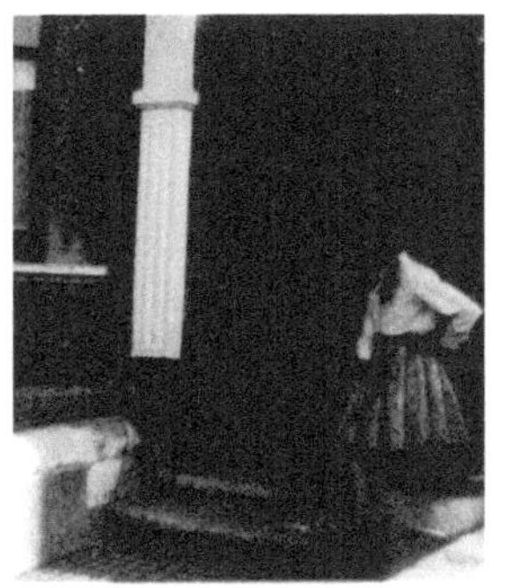

in love. It was here that the germ of my obsession quietly developed.

I thought running away was the answer. Running away was what I did best. My first home, idyllic in so many ways, imprinted so brightly on my young mind, vanished in the blink of an eye. The colours, however, remained imprinted. Mainly the brilliant blue of the ocean and the yellow of everyday. I took these with me to my second home with its endless talk of Western art. I found a painter I liked. He drew crows and because I had an intimate knowledge of crows, even at such a young age I liked this artist. Later I found out that he had been in love with a woman who had the same name as Ursula. I liked the painter even more because of this. And later still, when I saw how he used the colour blue, how he applied yellow on yellow, I thought I too might become a painter. Western art or art from other parts of the world, I hardly cared. I ground down some lapis and mixed turmeric with saffron. Then I used gum Arabic to bind the colours and began to paint. I admit the early paintings had room for improvement.

In my second home, there was no light here, only large plane trees and a private hedge that helped to block out the sun. That privacy was clearly more important than light was a concept that came to me only slowly.

I didn't hate the place, not straight away. Children don't process hate clearly when it comes to inanimate objects. They can hate other children or the cold but hating gloom was another matter. I couldn't say if I hated the apartment with all its deformed furniture but maybe my desire for beauty grew out of the strangeness of my new environment. Years later, if I thought of the house, it was always with a sense that the furniture in it, the heavy wardrobes, the ugly patterned carpets, were all simply waiting to be destroyed. That the building was a kind of graveyard, if I may use that expression, for the unwanted. Perhaps this was why, when asked after my mother died if there was anything I wanted, I simply shook my head.

'Get rid of it all,' I remember saying with a dismissive wave of my hand. The result was of course that I could never get rid of those things. They moved around in the rooms of my mind, arranging themselves to taunt my every waking hour. And in my sleep, they took on the characteristics of my parents themselves. These objects became, in short, *human*.

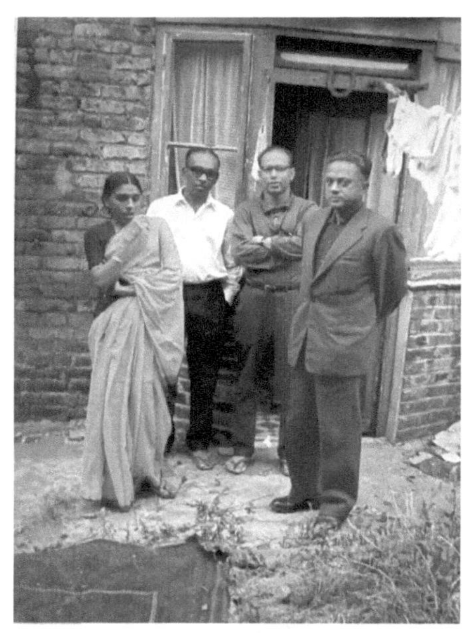

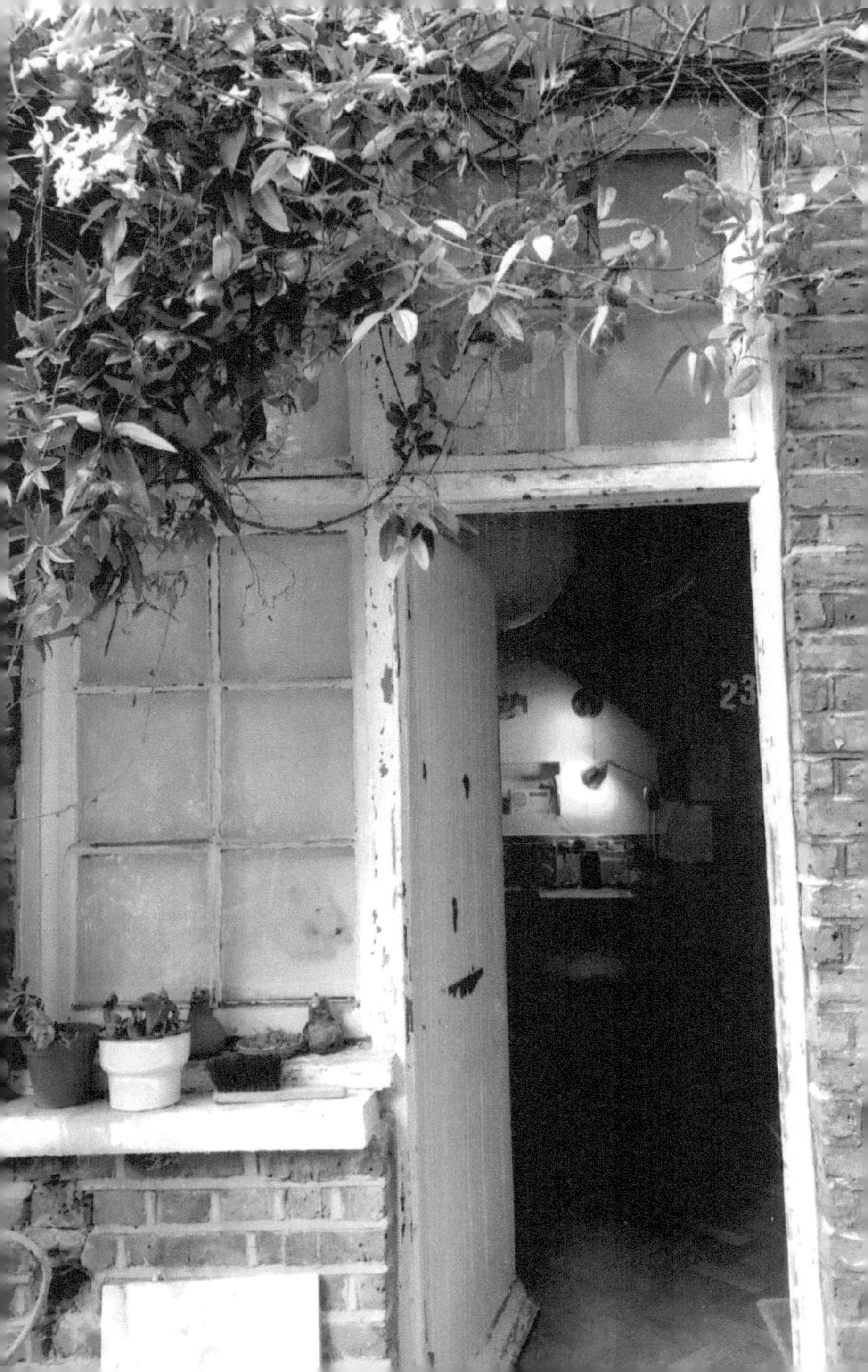

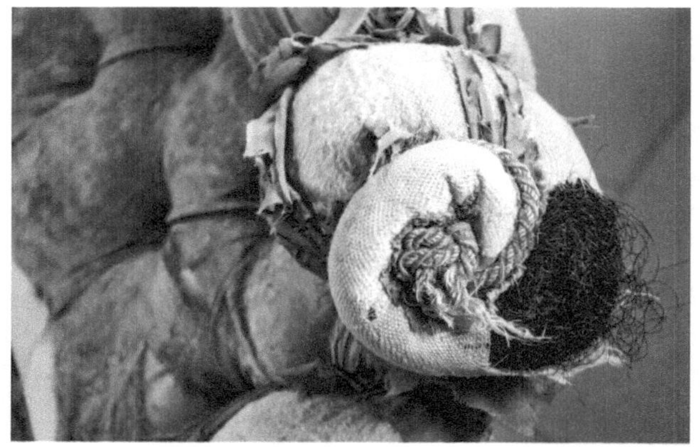

We rely on our past to define our
present. The aura of objects from days
gone by reaches out to us, defining
our relationships with our culture, our
friendships, even our own selves.

TRACe locates those links through
the many objects which make up its
collection, throwing a new light on the
living past within the present.

ISBN 978-1-912384-18-1

2nd edition. Published 2023.
by Peculiarity Press, an imprint of Leigh & Glennie Ltd.
Badgemore House, Badgemore Park, Henley-on-Thames, RG9 4NR, UK.
© Leigh & Glennie Ltd 2023.

Design by Jane Glennie. Typeset in Jenson family.

Peculiarity Press thanks the following for support:
James Gooch and Doe & Hope, Antonella Maione and KANZ Architetti,
Ulrike Leigh, Stephanie Nic Cárthaigh, Andrew Scrivens and Holmen
Paper, Phil Treble and Muttons & Nuts.

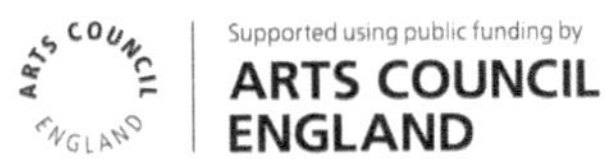

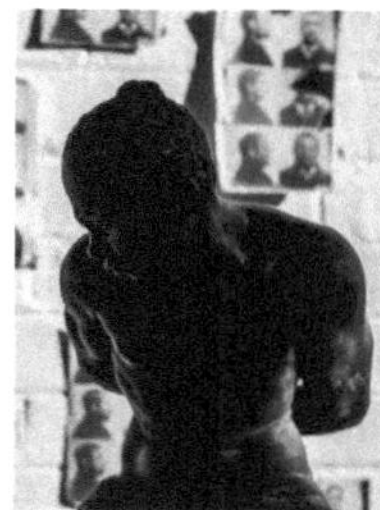